Recent Acquisitions

A SELECTION: 2000–2001

The Metropolitan Museum of Art

This publication was made possible
through the generosity of the
Lila Acheson Wallace Fund for
The Metropolitan Museum of Art
established by the cofounder of
Reader's Digest.

The Metropolitan Museum of Art Bulletin
Fall 2001
Volume LIX, Number 2 (ISSN 0026-1521)

Contents

General Manager of Publications: John P. O'Neill
Editor in Chief of the Bulletin: Joan Holt
Editor of the Bulletin: Jennifer Bernstein
Production: Peter Antony
Design: Bruce Campbell Design with
Bessas & Ackerman
Desktop Publishing Assistant: Minjee Cho

Coordinators: Mahrukh Tarapor and Sian Wetherill

All photographs, unless otherwise noted, are by the
Photograph Studio of The Metropolitan Museum
of Art. Photographers: Joseph Coscia Jr., Anna-
Marie Kellen, Paul Lachenauer, Oi-Cheong Lee,
Bruce Schwarz, Eileen Travell, Juan Trujillo,
Karin L. Willis, and Peter Zeray.

Director's Note

In the past few years a concerted effort has been made to augment the Metropolitan's funds for the acquisition of works of art. This *Bulletin* devoted to our recent acquisitions is testimony to the importance of that effort. There have been individual gifts, a number of them substantial, and the credit lines attached to major purchases record those donors' generosity and proclaim our gratitude. The Acquisitions Fund Benefit is now an annual tradition, and its proceeds allowed us last year to obtain an important seventeenth-century German sculpture by Leonhard Kern. In addition, the funds provided by several members of the Chairman's Council made possible the purchase of a splendid figure study by Sir Joshua Reynolds.

As in previous years, this issue of the *Bulletin* underscores the encyclopedic nature of the collections by nearly matching that diversity with newly acquired works spanning several millennia and continents. Once again, I would like to devote pride of place in this note

to Ambassador and Mrs. Walter Annenberg, whose continued munificence provides us this year with a number of important Impressionist and Post-Impressionist canvases, including two handsome Fantin-Latours. Our collection of nineteenth-century European paintings also benefited from the addition of its first work by the British/French landscape painter Richard Parkes Bonington, as well as of a unique and most touching painted document, Gauguin's portfolio of 1894 from his second Pont-Aven period. Mr. and Mrs. Leon Black are associated with the latter purchase, and it is my pleasure to observe here that their names are being linked to acquisitions with increasing frequency.

Among those groups of works of art that have measurably enhanced the quality and scope of other areas of the Museum's collections is the assemblage of "Dongson"-culture Bronze Age objects bequeathed by Samuel Eilenberg, which makes our holdings of this material virtually unrivaled in the Western

world; and the Fales Collection of American jewelry, which propels us to first rank in that field as well.

Finally, I wish to end by welcoming to the Museum a single work, one of the most important to be acquired in recent times by the Metropolitan in the field of African art: the large and imposing sculpture of a couple from the Menabe region of Madagascar. We could not have added this iconic image of man and woman to the collection without the assistance of valued friends of the Department of the Arts of Africa, Oceania, and the Americas. To these individuals, and to all the others who have contributed to the acquisitions program of the Museum in the past year—listed for the first time at the back of this *Bulletin*—I express my deepest gratitude. Their generosity is our lifeblood.

Philippe de Montebello
Director

Contributors

American Decorative Arts
North America 1700–1900: Morrison H. Heckscher (MHH), Lawrence A. Fleischman Chairman of the American Wing; Alice Cooney Frelinghuysen (ACF), Anthony W. and Lulu C. Wang Curator; Beth Carver Wees (BCW), Associate Curator; Medill Higgins Harvey (MH), Research Assistant.

American Paintings and Sculpture
North America 1700–1900: H. Barbara Weinberg (HBW), Alice Pratt Brown Curator; Carrie Rebora Barratt (CRB), Curator; Kevin J. Avery (KJA), Associate Curator. *Modern:* H. Barbara Weinberg (HBW).

Ancient Near Eastern Art
Ancient World: Joan Aruz (JA), Curator.

Arms and Armor
Renaissance and Baroque Europe: Stuart W. Pyhrr (SWP), Arthur Ochs Sulzberger Curator in Charge. *Asia:* Donald J. LaRocca (DJL), Curator.

Arts of Africa, Oceania, and the Americas
Africa, Oceania, and the Americas: Alisa LaGamma (AL), Associate Curator; Eric Kjellgren (EK), Evelyn A. J. Hall and John A. Friede Assistant Curator; Heidi King (HK), Senior Research Associate; Virginia-Lee Webb (VLW), Associate Research Curator, Photograph Study Collection.

Asian Art
Asia: James C. Y. Watt (JCYW), Brooke Russell Astor Chairman; Barbara B. Ford (BBF), Curator; Maxwell K. Hearn (MKH), Curator; Martin Lerner (ML), Curator; Suzanne G. Valenstein (SGV), Fellow; Steven M. Kossak (SMK), Associate Curator; Denise Patry Leidy (DPL), Associate Curator; Masako Watanabe (MW), Senior Research Associate.

Costume Institute
Modern: Harold Koda (HK), Curator in Charge. *Africa, Oceania, and the Americas:* Emily Martin (EM), Research Associate.

Drawings and Prints
Renaissance and Baroque Europe: Carmen C. Bambach (CCB), Associate Curator; Nadine M. Orenstein (NMO), Associate Curator; Michiel C. Plomp (MCP), Associate Curator; Perrin Stein (PS), Associate Curator; Elizabeth E. Barker (EEB), Assistant Curator. *Europe 1700–1900:* Colta Ives (CI), Curator; Elizabeth E. Barker (EEB). *Modern:* Colta Ives (CI); Samantha J. Rippner (SJR), Curatorial Assistant.

European Paintings
Renaissance and Baroque Europe: Keith Christiansen (KC), Jayne Wrightsman Curator; Walter Liedtke (WL), Curator; Mary Sprinson de Jésus (MSdJ), Research Fellow. *Europe 1700–1900:* Gary Tinterow (GT), Engelhard Curator of Nineteenth-Century European Painting; Susan Alyson Stein (SAS), Associate Curator. *Modern:* Gary Tinterow (GT).

European Sculpture and Decorative Arts
Renaissance and Baroque Europe: James David Draper (JDD), Henry R. Kravis Curator. *Europe 1700–1900:* James David Draper (JDD); Daniëlle O. Kisluk-Grosheide (DK-G), Associate Curator; Wolfram Koeppe (WK), Associate Curator; Jessie McNab (JMcN), Associate Curator; Jeffrey H. Munger (JHM), Associate Curator.

Greek and Roman Art
Ancient World: Carlos A. Picón (CAP), Curator in Charge; Joan R. Mertens (JRM), Curator; Christopher S. Lightfoot (CSL), Associate Curator; Seán Hemingway (SH), Assistant Curator.

Islamic Art
Islam: Daniel Walker (DW), Patti Cadby Birch Curator; Stefano Carboni (SC), Associate Curator; Navina Haidar (NH), Assistant Curator.

Medieval Art and The Cloisters
Ancient World: Melanie Holcomb (MH), Assistant Curator. *Medieval Europe:* Peter Barnet (PB), Michel David-Weill Curator in Charge; Barbara Drake Boehm (BDB), Curator; Timothy B. Husband (TBH), Curator; Charles T. Little (CTL), Curator; Julien Chapuis (JC), Associate Curator.

Modern Art
Europe 1700–1900: Sabine Rewald (SR), Associate Curator. *Modern:* Lisa M. Messinger (LMM), Associate Curator; Sabine Rewald (SR); Jane Adlin (JA), Assistant Curator; Jared Goss (JG), Assistant Curator; Anne L. Strauss (ALS), Assistant Curator; Nan Rosenthal (NR), Consultant; J. Stewart Johnson (JSJ), Consultant for Design and Architecture.

Musical Instruments
Europe 1700–1900: Herbert Heyde (HH), Associate Curator; Stewart S. Pollens (SSP), Associate Conservator. *North America 1700–1900:* Herbert Heyde (HH).

Photographs
Europe 1700–1900: Malcolm Daniel (MD), Associate Curator. *Modern:* Jeff L. Rosenheim (JLR), Assistant Curator; Douglas Eklund (DE), Research Associate; Mia Fineman (MF), Research Assistant.

2000.281.1

2000.281.2

2000.407.1, .2

Diadem, Brooch, and Armbands

Carpathian Basin (present-day Slovakia and Hungary), Late Bronze Age, 1200–900 B.C.
Copper alloy
Diam. (diadem) 10¼ in. (26 cm); l. (brooch)
11 in. (27.8 cm); l. (each armband) 9 in. (22.9 cm)
Purchase, Caroline Howard Hyman Gift,
in memory of Margaret English Frazer,
2000
2000.281.1, .2
Purchase, The Kurt Berliner Foundation
Gift, 2000
2000.407.1, .2

The elemental form of a spiral achieves an elegant monumentality in this diadem, large brooch, and pair of armbands. These remarkably whole pieces epitomize metallurgical production of the workshops found in the areas south of the Carpathian Mountains during the Late Bronze Age. In continental Europe no workshops were more prolific, creative, or technologically accomplished than these. The personal ornaments, weapons, and vessels they produced were widely imitated and exported and have been found in settlements as far away as Scandinavia, France, and Italy.

Though spirals had long figured in Bronze Age ornamentation, the workshops transformed what was a flat decorative motif into a sculptural shape for an array of jewelry that incorporated spirals. Often incised with delicate patterns of dots and lines, their products are noteworthy for the powerful, almost modern simplicity of their forms. Large brooches were worn by both men and women to secure cloaks, while diadems were probably worn only by women, with the spirals perhaps extending down at the back of the head. Armbands were usually worn in pairs on the lower arms; they were sometimes complemented by finger and toe rings, as well as by leg bands. It is impossible to say whether these imposing pieces were used exclusively for ceremonial purposes, but the rarity of their forms suggests the elite status of their original owners.

MH

Siren

Greek, Archaic period, ca. 550–500 B.C.
Terracotta
L. 9½ in. (24.1 cm)

Purchase, Renée E. and Robert A. Belfer Gift, 2000

2000.276

Part woman, part bird, this robust Archaic Greek sculpture represents a siren, a mythical creature famous in antiquity for its song that lured sailors off course to their deaths. In Greek mythology sirens, like harpies, embodied a potent aspect of feminine power. The wily hero Odysseus encountered them near their island in the Tyrrhenian Sea. By being lashed to the mast of his ship, Odysseus was able to hear the sirens' song without danger, while his crew plugged their ears so as not to be enchanted.

The geographer Strabo and other ancient writers tell us that sanctuaries dedicated to the sirens existed in parts of southern Italy and elsewhere. This sculpture may well have been a votive offering at such a sanctuary. Modeled by hand with applied decoration, it is much rarer than the mold-made, siren-shaped terracotta vessels that were popular throughout the Greek world during the Archaic period. It may also have been part of a sculptural group or have served as a crowning architectural element, possibly for a funerary monument, another context in which sirens frequently appear in Greek art.

SH

Support in the Shape of a Sphinx

Greek, ca. 600 B.C.
Bronze
H. 10⅞ in. (27.6 cm)

Gift from the family of Howard J. Barnet, in his memory, 2000

2000.660

Ancient literary sources and rare surviving objects testify to the monumental bronze utensils produced in Greece from the ninth to the sixth century B.C. This sphinx was one of the three—or more—supports that carried on their heads a shallow bronze basin measuring at least a meter in diameter. The hollow core of the piece is filled with lead, which helped to stabilize the utensil and, supplemented by rivets, held the various parts together. The sphinx has an elaborate coiffure with spiral curls over her forehead and tresses that fall behind her ears and widen in a succession of waves. A bolero-like arrangement of scales represents the feathers on her body and overlaps, in low relief, the flight feathers of her wings. She stands on a single feline paw, which is appropriate because a sphinx is part woman, part bird, and part lion. Among early utensil supports, female figures with demonic power are frequent; Gorgons rather than sphinxes predominate. Two hollows below the sphinx's wings indicate that originally she had a pair of arms or a second pair of wings, following Near Eastern prototypes.

JRM

Situla (Wine Bucket) with Two Handles

Greek, Hellenistic period, late 4th–early
3rd century B.C.
Glass and silver with gilding and paint
H. 8 in. (20.4 cm)
Purchase, The Bernard and Audrey
Aronson Charitable Trust Gift, in memory
of her beloved husband, Bernard Aronson,
2000

2000.277

This is an exceptional object by virtue of its
rarity, quality, technique, and decoration.
Prior to the invention of glassblowing in the
first century B.C. (a development that allowed
mass production), the finest glass vessels were
luxury objects. The bucket was manufactured
by casting a thick block of translucent green-
ish glass, which was then ground, polished,
painted, and gilded. The swing handles are
flat strips of silver.

The situla is an exceedingly rare shape in
the repertoire of Greek glassmakers. Even
more remarkable, however, is the painted
and gilded decoration that originally covered
most of the exterior. The ornament comprises
three main elements: A continuous wave pattern in pinkish red runs under the rim; two
broad vertical stripes with wavy tendrils in
purplish red descend the sides of the bucket

(there are traces of gilding over the paint in
the vertical bands); and the rest of the vessel's
body is largely covered with rows of assorted
floral or featherlike ornaments, painted in
several shades of pinkish red outlined with
dark brown. A pink rosette occupies the center of the situla's base. If the painted patterns
in fact represent overlapping feathers rather
than floral motifs, one could venture an
Egyptian origin for our glass bucket, since the
use of feathers to denote divinity has a long
history in Egyptian art.   CAP

Bracelet with Central Medallion

Greek, Hellenistic period, 2nd century B.C.
Gold and glass
Diam. 3⅜ in. (8.7 cm)
Purchase, The Concordia Foundation Gift
and Marguerite and Frank A. Cosgrove Jr.
Fund, 2001

2001.230

This gold bracelet is composed of two tubu-
lar sections hinged to an oval box bezel that
is embellished with a large purple glass cameo
with a white border. Gold pins secure the
collars of the two semicircular hoops. The
most distinctive feature of this well-preserved
bracelet (or armlet) is the treatment of the
outer surfaces of the hoops: They are covered
with a delicate network of filigree created by
placing parallel rows of wire in a zigzag pattern and dotting the points of contact with
granules. This unusual type of decoration
finds a close parallel in the three magnificent
gold bracelets (or torques) from the so-called
Karpenisi Treasure in Athens. Divided between
the National Archaeological Museum (Stathatos
Collection) and the Benaki Museum, this
famous Thessalian hoard has traditionally
been assigned to the second century B.C. In
terms of typology, our piece stands as a rare
Hellenistic forerunner of a popular kind of
Roman bracelet featuring twisted hoops and
hinged box settings decorated with gem-
stones, a fine example of which is owned by
the Metropolitan (acc. no. 1995.539.13).

CAP

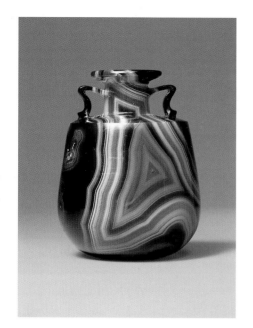

Amphora

Roman, 1st century B.C.–1st century A.D.
Banded agate
H. 2¼ in. (5.9 cm)
**Purchase, Mr. and Mrs. Sid R. Bass Gift,
in honor of Annette de la Renta, and
Rogers Fund, 2001**
2001.253

In Hellenistic and Roman times vessels made in semiprecious stone were much sought after as symbols of wealth and sophistication. Relatively few examples, however, have come down from antiquity; most of the surviving hard-stone vessels are small containers, such as this exquisite banded-agate amphora. Despite its small size, the vessel is a masterly example of the maker's skill. Not only does it have a pleasing shape and an attractive polished surface that shows off the patterning in the agate, but the carving out of the inside is also evidence of great technical dexterity.

Although gem-cutting workshops existed in Rome during the first century B.C., the techniques used to make such hard-stone bottles may be linked more closely to the production of luxury cast glassware. The establishment of such a glass industry in the imperial capital, probably during the Augustan period (27 B.C.–A.D. 14), may give support to the view that craftsmen making hard-stone vessels also migrated to that city, where the Roman aristocracy undoubtedly provided them with most of their business.

CSL

Chariot or Cart Trappings (?)

Provincial Roman, 2nd–3rd century A.D.
Copper alloy with champlevé enamel
Largest plaque 5⅝ × 3⅞ in. (14.3 × 9.7 cm)
**Purchase, Jeannette and Jonathan Rosen
Gift and Fletcher Fund, 2000**
2000.505a–o

This ensemble of champlevé-enamel plaques, remarkable for their vivid colors and exuberant presentation of classical motifs, attests to the skills of artists working in the outer reaches of the Roman Empire in the centuries of its greatest extent. The technique had long been a specialty of Celtic metalworkers, and it continued to develop independently of the great cities of the empire. Early enamels have been found in Britain, the northern Caucasus, southern Russia, and Syria, with the greatest concentration in Belgium and the Rhineland. Rome, a center of glassmaking, knew little of the art form. Indeed, one writer attached to the imperial court in the early third century marveled at the exotic ornaments fashioned with hardened colors by the "barbarians of the outer sea."

The precise function of this group is uncertain. The backs of nine plaques have projecting tangs that vary in their shape, size, and orientation. Short chains hanging from the sides distinguish one pair, while another pair sits atop a metal axle attached to wheel-like disks (bottom center). The quantity and hardware of the plaques suggest that they might have decorated a chariot or cart; such vehicles were often splendidly ornamented in the Roman world.   MH

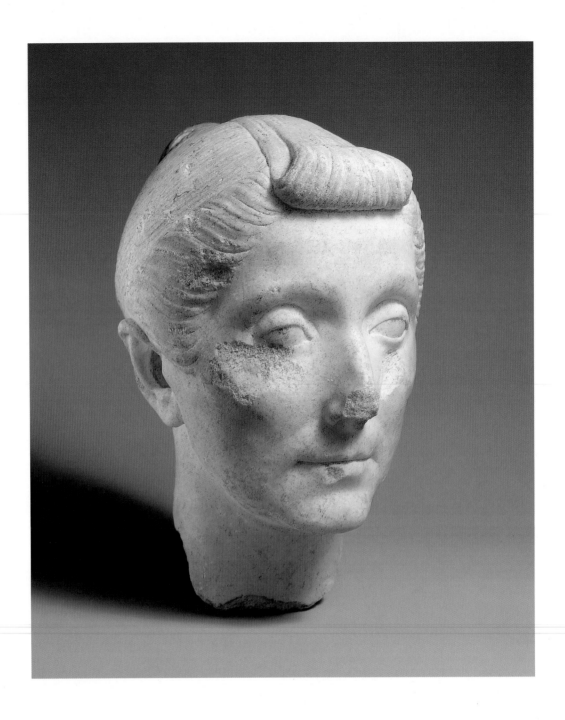

Portrait Head of a Roman Matron
Roman, ca. 40–20 B.C.
Marble
H. 10¼ in. (26 cm)
Purchase, Philodoroi Gifts, 2000
2000.38

This portrait conveys an air of *modestia* and *simplicitas* that is appropriate for its subject—an upper-class Roman matron. Such portraits are less common than those of Roman men. Like many others, however, this example can be closely dated by its hairstyle, known as the *nodus* (roll) coiffure, which became popular in Rome during the late first century B.C. Here the roll of hair above the forehead is combined with a bun worn at the back of the head in a markedly conservative mode. This old-fashioned hairstyle fits well with the portrait's visible signs of aging—sunken eyes,

slightly sagging skin at the jawline, and indentations at the corners of the mouth. Such details suggest that the sitter wanted to be seen as a traditional and virtuous Roman woman who dedicated herself to her home and family rather than to the latest dictates of high society. The sculpture retains traces of its original painted decoration, most notably on the right eye, where both the iris and the eyelashes are still visible. Brown pigment can also be seen on and around the bun. These features give the portrait an added interest, as it is highly unusual for painted details to survive.

CSL

Rhyton with Female Head

Probably Mesopotamia, late Parthian–early
Sasanian period, 3rd century A.D.
Glazed ceramic
H. 15 in. (38.1 cm)

Purchase, Gift of Dr. Mortimer D. Sackler,
Theresa Sackler and Family, and 2000
Benefit Fund, 2000

2001.178

This vessel belongs to a rare class of glazed
ceramic rhytons with female heads and
animal-shaped spouts. The upper part is in
the form of a vase with one handle (now
lost). It appears as a tall bulbous crown above
the head (made from two half-molds), which
displays puffy cheeks, thickly lined eyes and
brows, and small lips. The richly patterned
"melon" coiffure is embellished by a diadem
of wheat stalks with a band that includes a
palmette, a crescent and star, and a rosette.
Below a necklace the vessel tapers into a bull's
head with a pouring hole at the mouth.

The diadem motifs may identify the head
as that of the Mesopotamian goddess Nana,
daughter of the moon god and sister of the
sun god. This nature and astral deity—who is
referred to in texts from the Temple of Marduk,
Babylon, as "the power over princes and the
scepter of kings"—was represented in Parthian
and Kushan art and widely worshiped in Asia.
The vessel, a combination of an eastern
Mediterranean face pot and an Iranian animal-
head rhyton, may be compared to two similar
rhytons of unknown provenance with Sasanian-
style relief decoration (British Museum,
London, and Cincinnati Art Museum) and to
a molded female face on a late Parthian coffin
lid from Nippur (University of Pennsylvania
Museum of Archaeology and Anthropology,
Philadelphia).   JA

and the crescent attached to its collar. But the presence of S-spun linen (named for the direction of the twist, imparted in the process of forming a continuous thread from the fiber) virtually ensures that the textile is of Egyptian manufacture.

A repeat pattern such as the one we speculate existed on this piece was developed for drawloom weaving of luxury silks perhaps in the seventh century. Its appearance here in tapestry weave, in which repetition saves no time or labor, suggests that a Sasanian-style patterned silk served as a model for this early Islamic product of Egypt.

DW

Bowl

Western Asia, 9th century
Mosaic glass
Diam. 5½ in. (14 cm)
Rogers Fund, 2001
2001.266

This work was created in the mosaic technique by placing a number of small slices of glass canes next to one another to form a circle; fusing them into a disk at a high temperature; and finally slumping the disk over a curved, bowl-shaped mold. Each slice, cut from a long cane created by wrapping glass of different colors around a core, bears the pattern of a central red eye encircled in black and five red petals set against a yellow ground; the outer ring is of alternating yellow and green sections. During fusion the sliced canes became partially misshapen, creating a whimsical composition in which colors often run into one another—with brilliant translucent emerald green coming to life through transmitted light.

Mosaic glass is also known as *millefiori* ("thousand flowers") after its Venetian "reincarnation." The technique first appeared in Egypt about 1400 B.C.; then again in Rome and Alexandria during the second century B.C.; in Islamic Mesopotamia and Syria during the ninth century A.D.; and in Venice during the fifteenth century. Probably the longest and most successful period followed its reappearance during the first half of the nineteenth century in Venice, whence it spread throughout Europe, especially to France and to Bohemia, where the technique enjoys its greatest popularity today.

SC

Textile Fragment

Egypt, 8th century
Wool and linen; tapestry weave
H. 15⅛ in. (38.3 cm)
Louis E. and Theresa S. Seley Purchase Fund for Islamic Art and Dodge Fund, 2000
2000.668

This fragmentary textile has visual potency belying its modest dimensions. Probably originally one of a confronted pair, a horned ram with cameloid mouth and spotted coat stands in the lobed field of a circular roundel. It is likely that the roundel was one of many arranged in rows against the dark blue ground embellished with off-white scrolling vines.

Several features of this fragment are reminiscent of the art of Sasanian Iran produced during the centuries preceding the Arab conquest of 641, including the representation of an animal in a roundel, its fluttering scarf,

Fine ivory-inlaid furniture and related objects, such as this box, represented an active export market from Mughal India to Europe from the late sixteenth century onward. The production and trade of such furniture from the western coast of India was first related to demand in the Ottoman and Persian worlds, largely for mother-of-pearl and ivory settings in lac, and later was superseded in Europe by a market for inlay in hardwoods.

While many Europeanizing elements are evident in the decoration of the box, the idiom of a forest hunting scene is essentially a Mughal one. Such depictions of the chase found their ultimate inspiration in Persian compositions and later became a popular genre in Mughal painting. This box is related to a small but distinguished group of ivory-inlaid furniture—possibly produced in the same workshop—that includes a cabinet in the Museu Nacional de Arte Antiga, Lisbon, and a table cabinet in the Cincinnati Art Museum. The undulating branches of the bird-filled trees, against which lively figures of Portuguese hunters and animals have been set, make the box one of the most expressive and lyrical pieces of its type.

NH

Inlaid Box
India (Gujarat), Mughal period, Indo-Portuguese style, late 16th–early 17th century
Teak, ebony, ivory, and lac
L. 13½ in. (34.3 cm)
Cynthia Hazen Polsky and Leon B. Polsky Fund, 2000
2000.301

Black Stork in a Landscape

India (Lucknow), ca. 1780
Watercolor on European paper
29¾ × 21½ in. (75.6 × 54.6 cm)
Louis E. and Theresa S. Seley Purchase Fund for Islamic Art and Rogers Fund, 2000
2000.266

By the late eighteenth century many Mughal-trained painters in central and eastern India were looking to the emerging British ruling class for patronage. The products of this new Company School were often albums of flora, fauna, and other exotic sights of India, made to be taken back to Britain. Of the varied subjects, bird studies, such as this bold depiction of a sturdy black stork, may be deemed a classic type. Paintings of birds, animals, and flowers had been an important genre in Indian art since the time of the Mughal emperor Jahāngīr (r. 1605–27), and the continuation of such subjects under British patronage was a natural extension of that established tradition, although the results were often quite different stylistically.

In this painting the stork is standing upright in a receding landscape, of considerably reduced scale, that contains a meandering river. The dramatic contrast in size between the bird and the vista it dominates gives the composition a distinctively idiosyncratic mood. This effect is also seen in another, similar page depicting a hawk in a landscape, possibly from the same series, in the Binney Collection at the San Diego Museum of Art. While the background of the Metropolitan's picture is rendered in a washy application of paint, the bird itself has areas of dense color and fine brushwork.

NH

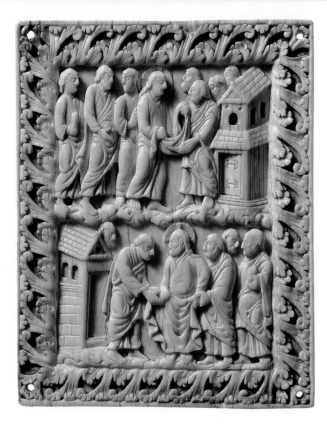

Two Scenes of Christ and Apostles
Carolingian (northern France), ca. 850–900
Ivory with traces of polychromy
3⅞ × 3⅛ in. (9.9 × 7.8 cm)
The Cloisters Collection, 2000
2000.486

In the age of Charlemagne and his successors biblical themes frequently conveyed political, moral, or ecclesiastical messages. This exquisite ivory carving portrays two unusual scenes focusing on Christ, the apostles, and a mantle. Since Christ traditionally wears only a tunic, he is presumably giving his mantle to an apostle in the presence of others. The episode does not seem to conform to a specific Gospel; it probably refers more generally to Christ's charge to his apostles to continue his ministry by accepting the mantle, or pallium, as an emblem of "apostolic mission" (Matthew 10:1–14). The message may also recall Isaiah (61:10), "my soul shall be joyful in my God;

for he hath clothed me with the garments of salvation . . . [and] with the robe of righteousness." A possible political sentiment may also be conveyed, as when Christ says, "they that wear soft clothing are in kings' houses" (Matthew 11:8). Probably made to decorate the cover of a liturgical manuscript, the ivory has striking narrative power. The narrow stage space, flowing groundline, and fleshy figures in garments with soft, curving edges exemplify some of the main stylistic trends of the second half of the ninth century associated with the court school of Charles the Bald (r. 840–77). The school's exact location in northern France is debated.

CTL

Cameo with the Fasting of Saint Nicholas
Southern Italian, 1200–1250
Agate with gold frame
H. 1 in. (2.5 cm)
Rogers Fund, 2000
2000.347

Court artists working for the German and Sicilian emperor Frederick II Hohenstaufen (1194–1250) excelled in the creation of exquisite cameos. Here a rare image of a saint depicts an episode from the infancy of Saint Nicholas, in which he refuses his mother's milk. Seated frontally and wearing a long tunic, she attempts to pull her nude son, who is seated sideways, toward her exposed breast. He refuses by grasping her hand. The theme is one known primarily in a monastic context, where it served as an exemplum for fasting and for abstinence.

The pendant must have had a personal significance for the owner, perhaps named Nicholas; whether the wearer was an ecclesiastic or a court figure is uncertain. As the relics of Saint Nicholas had resided at Bari, in Apulia, since the eleventh century, the protection of this important saint would have had wide appeal in Italy. Carved in a bold but precise hard-stone style, this is a rare and unrecorded cameo among the works produced in southern Italy during the remarkable reign of Frederick II, who revived antique traditions as part of his court culture.

CTL

Prophet King from a Tree of Jesse Window
German (Saxony or Thuringia [possibly Wurzen]), 1260–70
Pot-metal glass with vitreous paint
9⅛ × 9⅛ in. (23.2 × 23.2 cm)
The Cloisters Collection, 2000
2000.406

This half-length figure of a prophet king almost certainly came from a Tree of Jesse window that incorporated scenes from the Infancy of Christ, four panels of which are now installed in Falkenstein Castle, in the Harz Mountains near Germany's border with the Czech Republic. The original location of the window is uncertain, but it may have come from the church in Wurzen, east of Leipzig, in the diocese of Meissen. Although the window appears to have been made in the eastern reaches of Germany (Sachsen-Anhalt), the king depicted is stylistically similar to works from the Rhineland. The panel is an eloquent and crisp expression of the "zigzag" style (*Zackenstil*), characterized by sharply angled and hooked lines, that is a hallmark of both manuscript and panel painting in the mid- and late thirteenth century; the period was heretofore unrepresented in our holdings of German stained glass. With its strong affinities to the Aschaffenburg Evangelary (Aschaffenburg, Hofbibliothek ms. 13), this work also convincingly underscores the close relationship between manuscript illumination and glass painting in this period and the consequent dissemination of styles.   TBH

Cup with Trefoil Handle
Bohemian (Prague), 3rd quarter of 14th century
Jasper with silver-gilt mount and foot
H. 4⅛ in. (10.4 cm)
Purchase, Mrs. Charles Wrightsman Gift, in honor of Annette de la Renta, 2000
2000.504

With its integrally carved trefoil handle, deep dodecahedral bowl, and massive gilt mounts, this cup is as rare as it is spectacular. There are few surviving examples of Western medieval lapidary. Indeed, medieval European vessels carved from semiprecious stone are so little known that preserved examples are sometimes mistakenly attributed to the imperial courts of Rome and Byzantium. The confusion is one that would have delighted the cup's creators.

Carved from a material that is immediately perceived as precious and exotic, the vessel is a product of the imperial court of Charles IV (crowned at Rome 1355; d. 1378). Its jasper, with characteristic amethyst inclusions, could have been mined only in the foothills of the Ore Mountains, northwest of Prague. A sixteenth-century source tells of the emperor's sending men there to search for semiprecious stones to decorate his cathedral and royal chapel. In recent years geologists have found traces of their work in abandoned shafts dating to the Middle Ages tucked into the mountains near Ciboušov. Today Bohemian jasper still sheathes the chapel walls at Prague Cathedral and at Karlstejn Castle, just outside the city. Often vessels of this period have lost their original mounts or have been embellished by subsequent owners. The Museum's cup, remarkably, retains its medieval mount, which bears comparison to goldsmiths' work created in Prague and preserved in the cathedral treasury.

BDB

Giovanni di Balduccio
Italian (Tuscany, Bologna, and Milan), active 1318–49
Relief with Saint Peter Martyr and Three Donors
Ca. 1340
Marble
31½ × 33⅞ in. (80 × 86 cm)
The Cloisters Collection, 2001
2001.221

Trained in Pisa, Giovanni di Balduccio is noted for bringing the innovations of Tuscan sculptors to northern Italy. With quiet monumentality, this panel depicts the standing image of the bearded Saint Peter Martyr (d. 1252) wearing Dominican garb. The head wound, his primary attribute, is clearly visible along with a (restored) palm of martyrdom in his right hand. The saint's cloak, held open by his outstretched arms, frames three praying donor figures, while he places his hands on the heads of the oldest and the youngest of them. This relief is carved in a white fine-grained marble set into a frame of slightly coarser, grayer marble.

The sculpture is one of three marble panels to survive from a tomb originally in the Milanese church of Sant'Eustorgio. The

damaged central panel (Castello Sforzesco, Milan) depicts the Enthroned Virgin and Child between two angels, and the relief originally on the viewer's left (Sant'Eustorgio, Milan) shows Saint John the Baptist with four kneeling donors in a composition that mirrors the Museum's panel, which must have been on the right. Details such as the molding beneath the ledge supporting the figures and the buttons on the undersides of the sleeves suggest that the reliefs were intended to be above eye level.

PB

Pilgrim's Badge Depicting the Shrine of Saint Thomas Becket at Canterbury Cathedral

English, 1350–1400
Pewter
H. 3⅛ in. (7.9 cm)
Gift of Dr. and Mrs. W. Conte, 2001
2001.310

The brutal murder of Archbishop Thomas Becket in Canterbury Cathedral on December 29, 1170, transformed him into one of the most venerated saints in Western Christendom, and his shrine instantly became a pilgrimage site. This impressed badge shows the shrine of the martyred saint before it was plundered by Henry VIII's commissioners in 1538. The golden structure, as seen on the badge, was ordered by Archbishop Thomas Langton and dedicated on July 7, 1220. Created by the famed goldsmith Walter of Colchester, the tomb, supported on four bays, contained an effigy of Thomas Becket in ecclesiastical vestments. Here, raised above it, is the gabled shrine, encrusted with jewels on a trellislike ground and surmounted by two ship models, one of which is damaged. A small figure points to a ruby, claimed to be the largest in existence and given in 1179 by the king of France. To the right another figure raises the cover of the shrine with ropes and a pulley. This badge is one of the best surviving visual documents of the shrine. Its

accuracy is attested to by descriptions from ambassadors, clergy, and theologians, such as Erasmus. The badge is an important addition to our knowledge of the imagery surrounding this martyr-saint and joins our unrivaled collection of objects associated with him.

CTL

Pietà (Vesperbild)

Bohemian, ca. 1400

Limestone

H. 15 in. (38.1 cm)

The Cloisters Collection, 2001

2001.78

Images of the Virgin with the dead Christ reflect late-medieval trends in mysticism that encouraged a direct emotional response to biblical stories. Created as an object of private devotion, this group is a strikingly pure expression of the *Schöne Stil* (Beautiful Style), an artistic idiom that emerged at the imperial court in Prague at the end of the fourteenth century and subsequently resonated in artistic centers throughout Europe. The sculptor exploited the formal and psychological tensions inherent in the composition, combining a precise rendering of detail with a selectively abstract treatment of surfaces. Christ's broken, emaciated body, naked except for the loincloth, offers a stark contrast to the Virgin's youthful figure, clad in abundant folds. The high quality of the execution is evident in such details as the minutely striated loincloth and head veil; the vital delineation of Christ's arms, in which sinews and veins are visible; and the three intertwined hands, entirely undercut, on the Virgin's lap. The blending of sensuality and restraint gives this sculpture immediate emotional appeal.

JC

Master of the Berswordt Altar

German (Westphalian), active ca. 1400–1435

The Flagellation

Ca. 1400

Tempera and gold on wood

22¾ × 16⅞ in. (57.8 × 42.9 cm)

Bequest of Hertha Katz, 2000

2001.216.2

This is one of eighteen scenes that formed the interior wings of the Bielefeld Altarpiece, which was intact in the Neustädter Marienkirche, Bielefeld, until the church was restored in about 1840. The central panel, a Glorification of the Virgin flanked by twelve scenes, is shown to this day on the church's main altar. As they were originally displayed, the scenes comprised an extensive narrative sequence, beginning with the Fall of Man, followed by the lives of the Virgin and of Christ, and concluding with the Last Judgment. *The Flagellation* joins a Crucifixion, also from the Bielefeld wings, that the Museum purchased in 1943 (acc. no. 43.161) and that would have followed closely upon the Flagellation in the story of the life of Christ. Three other scenes from the interior wings are preserved in a private collection, Bielefeld, and single panels are in the Oetker Museum, Bielefeld; the Gemäldegalerie, Berlin; and the Ashmolean Museum, Oxford.

The artist is named after a triptych of 1431 (Marienkirche, Dortmund) that bears the coat of arms of the Berswordt family. As seen here, his work reflects the influence of the better-known German Gothic painters Master Bertram (active by 1367– d. 1414/15) and Conrad von Soest (ca. 1360– after 1422) and exemplifies the mannered refinement of late Gothic painting on the eve of the Renaissance.

MSDJ

Leonardo da Vinci

Italian, 1452–1519

Studies for the Movements of Water, Male Nude Unsheathing a Sword, and Hercules Holding a Club Seen in Frontal View (recto)
Study for Hercules Holding a Club Seen in Rear View (verso)

1506–8

Charcoal or soft black chalk, pen and dark brown ink (recto); charcoal or soft black chalk (verso); on off-white laid paper

5⅜ × 5½ in. (13.7 × 14 cm)

Purchase, Florence B. Selden Bequest and Rogers Fund, and Promised Gift of Leon D. and Debra R. Black, 2000

2000.328a, b

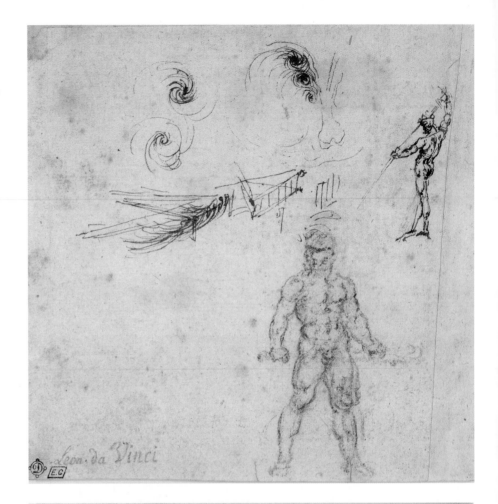

Most likely a cropped page from a notebook, this sheet vividly illustrates the parallel paths of Leonardo's artistic and scientific genius. The recto depicts at the top three sketches of the centrifugal swirling movement of water around obstacles (probably the thin wood piers of a bridge). Below are a view of water flowing by a wood bridge and, to the right, a slender nude man unsheathing a sword. At the bottom the classical hero Hercules is seen from the front holding a club. On the verso Hercules is shown from the rear.

The sheet can be dated to 1506–8, shortly after Leonardo stopped work on the *Battle of Anghiari* cartoon and mural for the Great Council Hall of the Palazzo Vecchio, Florence. The drawings of Hercules were apparently intended for an unexecuted statue. In representing him holding the club horizontally, Leonardo reinvented Hercules as an icon of preparedness, not unlike the symbolic allusion to civic vigilance evoked in Michelangelo's monumental marble *David* of 1501–4 (Gallerie dell'Accademia, Florence), which at the time was placed at the entrance of the Palazzo Vecchio. Considering the spirited professional interaction between the two artists during these years, it may well be that Leonardo conceived of his Hercules with a public function in mind and in competition with Michelangelo's *David*.

CCB

Hans Holbein the Younger
German, 1497/98–1543
Saint Thomas
1527
Pen and black ink, brush and gray wash,
heightened with white, on washed-brown paper
8 × 4⅛ in. (20.4 × 10.5 cm)
Purchase, Pat and John Rosenwald Gift,
Rogers Fund, and Gift of Dr. Mortimer D.
Sackler, Theresa Sackler and Family, 2001
2001.188

Holbein was one of the most versatile German artists to emerge after Dürer's maturity
(attained ca. 1500). Active as a painter and
draftsman, he also produced designs for
prints, metalwork, stained glass, and jewelry.
This sheet—the first work on paper by Holbein
the Younger to enter the Museum's collections—belongs to a series of drawings of the
apostles in the same size, medium, and technique. In all likelihood they were meant as
independent, finished works. Several, like
Saint Thomas, are dated 1527 and thus origi-
nate from Holbein's first English period,
where they form an isolated but striking example of religious work made at that point
in the artist's career.

MCP

Despite its apparent simplicity, *Mary Magdalen* is one of Master i.e.'s most accomplished works. He depicted the patron saint of hair-dressers and perfumers as a graceful, pensive figure clothed in an elegant robe, with her hair tied in large braids around her head. She delicately grasps her attribute, the jar contain-ing the ointment with which she anointed Christ's feet. The depiction of the saint as a single figure, removed from any narrative and standing on a schematically indicated mound of earth, is related to prints by the great fifteenth-century northern European printmaker Martin Schongauer, but Master i.e. depicted his saint on a much larger scale and rendered the costume with an intricate brocade seldom seen in his teacher's work.

We know very little about the author of this beautiful engraving. He was most likely active in the shop of Martin Schongauer, to whom much of his work is stylistically indebted. Our name for this unknown artist derives from an interpretation of the Gothic initials that appear in reverse on an engraving of a peasant holding a sausage (unique impres-sion in the Kupferstichkabinett, Staatliche Museen zu Berlin) and that may or may not be his monogram; none of the other prints attributed to him is signed.

NMO

Here Gossaert depicted the Holy Family sit-ting on a bench next to a tree, of which we can see only the trunk. The Virgin Mary dandles the naked Christ child on her lap as he turns his head to look at us. Next to them is Joseph, who offers Mary a flower. Gossaert paid a great deal of attention to the drapery folds. Their detailed execution and almost sculptural quality are in contrast to the sketchier, less-worked-out figures. In the background faint lines seem to indicate first thoughts for a possible architectural setting. The exquisite drawing might have been a pre-liminary study for an unidentified painting or print. Another possibility might be that the drawing was meant to be an independent work, but for an unknown reason the artist left it unfinished. MCP

This recently discovered sheet is a rare work by Jean Cousin the Elder, one of the most original and appealing artists of the French Renaissance. He was active as a designer of tapestry, stained glass, and book illustrations, as well as of ephemeral festival decorations for the French court. Nonetheless, Cousin's oeuvre has proved difficult to reconstruct, as the majority of his designs are known only through the final products executed by skilled artisans in other media. This is one of a small number of firmly autograph sheets by his hand. It is connected to a set of eight tapestries (three survive) illustrating the life of Saint Mamas, commissioned in 1543 for the cathedral at Langres.

Saint Mamas was an obscure child martyr who lived in Cappadocia during the third century. He was born in prison to a mother who died just after his birth; his father had died just before it. A local widow, Amya, was instructed by a divine vision to petition the governor for permission to adopt the child and to give his parents a Christian burial. The lost tapestry for which this is a study presumably would have been the first in the series.

PS

Maarten van Heemskerck
Netherlandish, 1498–1574
Man Protected by the Shield of Faith
1559
Pen and brown ink, over traces of black chalk,
on paper; indented for transfer
14⅜ × 10¼ in. (36.4 × 25.9 cm)
Purchase, Jessie H. Price and Guy
Wildenstein Gifts, Fletcher Fund, and
Gift of Dr. Mortimer D. Sackler,
Theresa Sackler and Family, 2000
2000.150

Maarten van Heemskerck, a Netherlandish
artist who stayed several years in Rome
(1532–36), became widely known throughout
Europe from the nearly six hundred prints
made after his designs. The present sheet is
an exceptionally fine example of his drafts-
manship, with a daring diagonal composition
in which the figures are in full motion. They
reveal his admiration for classical sculpture
and paintings by Michelangelo and Giulio
Romano. A praying man, confronted by

the temptations of worldliness (symbolized
by the globe) and by the Seven Deadly Sins
(represented on the scalloped edge of the
rug), is protected from Satan's burning
arrows by the female personification of faith.
Van Heemskerck may have developed the
unusual subject in collaboration with the
printmaker and religious philosopher Dirck
Volckertsz. Coornhert (1522–1590), who
engraved the design for publication.

MCP

26

Pompeo della Cesa

Italian, active ca. 1565–1600

Portions of an Armor for Vincenzo Luigi di Capua, Prince of Riccia

Milan, ca. 1595

Steel, gold, leather, and brass

H. 19 in. (48 cm)

Purchase, Arthur Ochs Sulzberger Gift, 2001

2001.72

Italian armor making in the last quarter of the sixteenth century was dominated by Pompeo della Cesa, armorer to the Spanish court in Milan. His richly decorated harnesses were coveted by Philip II of Spain, the ruling dukes of Savoy, Parma, and Mantua, and the scions of the leading Spanish and Italian families. Pompeo was one of the few armorers who regularly signed his pieces, a reflection of his pride of workmanship and his elevated status in the world of military *alta moda*.

Vincenzo Luigi di Capua (d. 1627), prince of Riccia, belonged to an ancient Neapolitan family. Don Vincenzo's armor, made shortly after he succeeded to his noble titles in 1594, exemplifies Pompeo's best work. The surfaces are covered with closely set vertical bands etched with trophies of arms, religious and allegorical figures, and grotesques, all partly gilt. The owner's emblem, or *impresa,* appears at the top of the breastplate—a radiant sun with a crown above and a motto below, NVLLA QVIES ALIBI (No repose but here); Pompeo's name is etched beneath. Now incomplete, the half-length infantry armor originally included an open-faced helmet and arm defenses. The matching backplate is preserved in Warwick Castle, England.

SWP

Detail

of prints was far-ranging, offering a view into life in the seventeenth-century duchy of Lorraine—from the pomp of court pageants to the miseries of war. Depictions of horses were central to images of both celebrations and battles. Callot's studies explore not only equine anatomy but also the potential of drawing to imbue a two-dimensional image with a living, breathing vitality—a remarkable achievement when one realizes that he worked not from life but from the more static medium of prints. Exploiting the speed of the pen and the organic swelling and tapering of the ink line, Callot created an effective analogy to the power and grace of this majestic animal, so important to seventeenth-century life.

PS

Jacques Callot
French, 1592–1635
Study of a Horse
Ca. 1616
Quill and reed pen and iron gall ink on off-white laid paper; evidence of leadpoint or graphite tracing of standing horse on recto
9¼ × 11¼ in. (23.5 × 28.6 cm)
Promised Gift of Mr. and Mrs. David M. Tobey, and Purchase, Mr. and Mrs. David M. Tobey Gift, 2000
2000.253a, b

This two-sided sheet is part of a group of spirited studies of horses made during Callot's sojourn (ca. 1612–21) at the Medici court in Florence. Youthful works, they take their inspiration from a series of etchings by Antonio Tempesta, *Cavalli di differenti paesi,* published in Rome in 1590. Unlike the majority of Callot's extant drawings, they were not directly preparatory for prints but presumably remained in the artist's studio as a resource for his later work.

The subject matter of Callot's vast corpus

Scarsellino (Ippolito Scarsella)
Italian (Ferrarese), ca. 1550–1620
The Virgin Adored by Saints
Ca. 1609
Oil on copper
19¼ × 29¼ in. (48.9 × 74.3 cm)
Gift of Mary Jane Harris, in memory of Morton B. Harris and in honor of Keith Christiansen, 2001
2001.417

This beautifully preserved picture shows the Virgin bestowing the scapular—a small piece of cloth symbolic of one's having taken on the "yoke of Christ"—upon a saint, presumably Simon Stock, the thirteenth-century English Carmelite friar who had a vision of this occurrence. Two donors kneel in the left middle distance with Saint Anthony of Padua. Among those also present are Saints Catherine of Siena; Dominic, accompanied by a dog holding a long taper in its mouth; Nicholas of Tolentino; Francis of Assisi, preaching to birds on the nearby bluff; and Raymond of Peñaforte, sailing across the sea on a billowing banner. The Feast of the Scapular was established in 1609, and the picture must date to about that time.

Though underappreciated today, Scarsellino was admired by his contemporaries. Giulio Mancini—that extraordinary physician and dilettante whose writings are so important for the study of seventeenth-century painting—considered him "among the best living masters in Italy." Scarsellino owed the color and refined naturalism of his paintings largely to Paolo Veronese, with whom he worked in Venice. This picture seems also to demonstrate his awareness of the innovations of the Carracci in Bologna.

KC

Jan Brueghel the Elder
Flemish, 1568–1625
Landscape with Travelers on a Woodland Road
Ca. 1605–10
Oil on copper
3¾ × 6 in. (9.5 × 15.2 cm)
Bequest of Hertha Katz, 2000
2001.216.1

In the early 1600s Jan Brueghel was one of the most inventive masters of landscape painting in the Netherlands. The Antwerp artist had the considerable advantage of following in his famous father's footsteps; Pieter Bruegel the Elder, who died when Jan was one year old, passed on his vision of nature mainly through drawings. Jan himself sketched numerous studies of forests, fields, rivers, ordinary figures, and animals, as is evident from the few drawings by him in the Museum's collection.

Collectors in cities such as Antwerp, Frankfurt, Prague, and Rome embraced the latest examples of close observation, whether of flowers (in which Brueghel also excelled) or of extensive terrain, not only for their empirical approach but also as marvels of artistic invention and skill. It is in the context of discerning connoisseurship that Brueghel's miniature cabinet pictures may be best appreciated. A patron such as Brueghel's devoted supporter Cardinal Federigo Borromeo would have noted that the artist's subtle powers of description, as found in the Museum's comparatively large panel of 1607, *A Woodland Road with Travelers* (acc. no. 1974.293), seem unimpeded by concentration on a small scale. In this diminutive picture the endless flow of life in the Flemish countryside appears reproduced in microcosm.

WL

Peter Paul Rubens
Flemish, 1577–1640
A Sermon in a Village Church
1630s
*Black chalk, brush and brown-red ink,
watercolor, and gouache on paper*
16 ⅝ × 22½ in. (42.2 × 57.3 cm)
Harris Brisbane Dick Fund, 2000
2000.483

With great facility and virtuosity Rubens
depicted what appears to be a straightforward
genre scene of a village sermon. A congregation of farmers and peasants—men on the
left and women on the right—listens with
varying degrees of attentiveness to a sermon
offered by a potbellied minister standing in a
pulpit. It has been suggested that the drawing
represents a gathering on Rubens's estate in
Flanders and that the congregation may be
made up, at least in part, of his employees at
the Château de Steen. In the 1630s Rubens
painted and drew peasants much more often
than before, probably deliberately pursuing
Pieter Bruegel the Elder's tradition of
peasant depictions.   MCP

Charles Beale II
British, 1660–1714
Carter, the Colorman
*Red chalk, heightened with touches of black
chalk, on paper*
10¼ × 8 in. (26 × 20.3 cm)
**Purchase, Charles and Jessie Price Gift,
2001**
2001.121

Charles Beale II's remarkable red-chalk studies of family members and friends, although
not intended for a public audience, comprise
his most distinguished legacy. Beale's intimate
subjects—compelling for their immediacy
and for their vigorous cross-hatching in

waxy red chalk strengthened with black chalk and graphite—are virtually unique in British art of the late Stuart period and rank among its finest achievements. The present sheet once belonged to a sketchbook (British Museum, London) that is inscribed on the flyleaf, "Charles Beales 3d Book, 1680." It depicts a certain Carter (active 1680–1742), a purveyor of artists' materials, whom Beale drew on several occasions. Here the artist contrasts the tight, incisive strokes of red chalk that describe the contours of the young man's head to the more loosely sketched cravat and shirt, which appear to melt into the expansive white sheet. EEB

Leonhard Kern

German, 1588–1662

The Deposition

Ca. 1640–50

Alabaster

H. 12⅞ in. (32.7 cm)

Signed (lower left) with monogram

Purchase, 2000 Benefit Fund, 2000

2000.283

Despite the ravages of the Thirty Years' War, Leonhard Kern's shop in Schwäbisch Hall flourished, producing statuettes and small reliefs of high quality in boxwood, ivory, and alabaster. This output extended the precepts of Renaissance art well into the seventeenth century, thanks to Kern's memories of his study in Italy (1609–12) and his emulation of famous Italian masters such as Giovanni Bologna. To the latter he may owe the V-shaped cleft in the mountains that part in this scene to reveal Jerusalem and enframe the Holy Women (above center), as well as the rectilinear cluster of figures at right that includes Joseph of Arimathea, carrying a stack of linens and directing the preparation of Christ's body for burial. Yet these are not strict quotations, and the design, characteristically for Kern, is full of original touches, especially the angel at center—rare to this episode—who serves as intermediary between God and man and whose wings greatly activate the composition.

JDD

Decorative Ewer
Possibly Flemish, 1st half of 18th century
Alder wood
H. 33½ in. (85.1 cm)
**Purchase, Friends of European Sculpture
and Decorative Arts Gifts, 2000**
2000.492

Composed of several pieces of alder wood, this highly inventive ewer, with its slender neck, double handle, and exuberant spout, is a marvel of virtuoso carving. Following the tradition of designs for ornamental vases by seventeenth-century artists such as the French engraver Jean le Pautre and the Netherlandish engraver Claes Jansz. Visscher, the ewer's profile is enveloped by a multiplicity of decorative elements. The putti, garlands of fruit and flowers, and large sinuous foliage recall the spirited and fluid style of Flemish carving as expressed in elaborate sculpted pulpits and the balustrades of grand staircases. The reclining figure in the center (detail), crowned with vines, and his female companion may well be Bacchus, god of wine, and Ceres, goddess of agriculture, while the playful putti on the sides may allude to Venus. If so, the ewer could illustrate the saying "Sine Cerere et Baccho, friget Venus," implying that without food and drink, love is left out in the cold. The ewer has not yet yielded all its secrets: Was it, for instance, part of a larger decorative ensemble for a stately dining room, or perhaps a model to be executed in silver? Also, the identity of *Henricus Ioseph W [. . .],* inscribed in ink underneath the base, is not known.

DK-G

Detail

Jug

French (Saint-Cloud), ca. 1730–35
Soft-paste porcelain
H. 3½ in. (8.9 cm)
The Charles E. Sampson Memorial Fund, 2000
2000.174

Soft-paste porcelain was first produced commercially in France in the 1690s at a faience factory in Saint-Cloud, a small town west of Paris. The factory began by copying porcelains imported from China, but it soon developed its own distinctive style, which was entirely French in character. Much of the factory's production concentrated upon wares decorated with complex patterns painted in a deep cobalt blue. However, in the 1720s it began experimenting with ground colors, notably green and yellow. The overglaze yellow ground, derived from Chinese ceramics, proved difficult to master technically, and surviving examples of it are rare.

This small jug, which probably dates to the early 1730s, displays the difficulties that the factory was still experiencing at that time with the yellow ground. The color is uneven in thickness and has bonded poorly to the porcelain body in numerous places. Despite its flaws, the jug must have been perceived as highly original when it was produced.

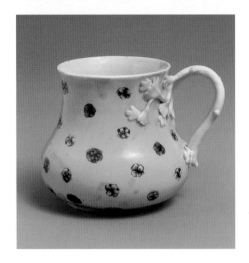

The use of European flowers scattered on a Chinese-style yellow ground resulted in a type of decoration that was completely novel in Continental porcelain.

JHM

Tobacco Pipe with Original Case

South German, ca. 1740
Silver, antler, horn, and leather
L. (pipe) 15⅜ in. (39.2 cm)
Purchase, Rogers Fund, and Bequest of Irwin Untermyer and funds from various donors, by exchange, 2001
2001.353a–c

The deformed, roselike base of a roebuck antler was mounted in silver to form this pipe's bowl. Remarkable is the use of the Y-shaped prong finial that teasingly evokes smoke coming out of the perforated silver lid. The arched silver tube decorated with applied antler was inspired by an oriental hookah. The bowl's exotic appearance resembles the ornamental Chinese scholars' rocks and the flamboyant rock formations found in Chinese gardens, both widely admired in the West. The silver *rocaille* mounts echo and complement the antler deformations, thus exemplifying the interplay of art and nature. In eighteenth-century Europe the hunting of stags was a strongly guarded, aristocratic privilege. Therefore this sublime oddity was most likely made for a princely curiosity cabinet (*Kunstkammer*), a room where such objects could be handled and studied from every angle.

Tobacco was considered to have aphrodisiac powers, and pulverized stag horn was thought to enhance strength. These attributes—together with the shell shape of the bowl's silver bottom, which refers to Venus, the goddess of love—could offer opportunities for initiating provocative conversations. The pipe is a Rococo document par excellence, both for its taste of the bizarre and for the mounting of highly treasured natural substances with precious metal.

WK

Sir Joshua Reynolds
British, 1723–1792
Study of a Woman and Child
Black chalk on off-white laid paper
10½ × 7¼ in. (26.6 × 18.3 cm)
Purchase, several members of The Chairman's Council Gifts, 2000
2000.285

Reynolds—the first president of the Royal Academy, an influential theoretician of art, and a prominent collector—was the leading British portraitist of the late eighteenth century. This study is not related to any known painting, but the canonical arrangement of the figures (here alluding to the Madonna and child) and the elegant, classicizing style (evidently inspired by the example of Michelangelo) are characteristic of Reynolds's most accomplished Grand Manner portraits of the 1770s. He may have presented the sheet directly to its earliest recorded owner, the first earl of Warwick, an important patron for whom Reynolds prepared at least seven portraits.

Distinguished by its fluent and incisive quality of line, *Study of a Woman and Child* ranks among the finest figure drawings by Reynolds and complements the Museum's eleven portraits by the artist and a sketchbook from his Italian journey of 1750–52.

EEB

Benedetto Pistrucci
Italian, 1783–1855
Proof Sovereigns of George III
British (London, Royal Mint), 1817 and 1820
Gold
Diam. (each) ⅞ in. (2.2 cm)
Gift of Assunta Sommella Peluso, Ada Peluso, and Romano I. Peluso, in memory of Ignazio Peluso, 2000
2000.224.4, .5

The Metropolitan has not been known historically for collecting coins, but the Peluso family's gift of British coinage is a worthy addition for its revelations of high artistry. Benedetto Pistrucci began his career in Rome, carving cameos with amazing dexterity. Soon after his arrival in London in 1815, he became chief engraver at the Royal Mint. The coins of George III (r. 1760–1820) are among the most elegant ever created. (The obverse of one specimen and the reverse of another are illustrated.) The gold sovereign's obverse succinctly invests the fat, ancient monarch with authority, while the reverse, with Saint George and the Dragon encircled in the Order of the Garter, is so successful in its clarity that it has been repeated (minus the Order) on the specie of most succeeding British monarchs.

JDD

Richard Parkes Bonington
British, 1802–1828
View near Rouen
Ca. 1825
Oil on millboard
11 × 13 in. (27.9 × 33 cm)
**Purchase, Gift of Joanne Toor Cummings,
by exchange, 2001**
2001.45

Although Bonington was born in England, he moved to France with his parents in 1818 and enrolled in the Paris studio of Baron Gros in 1820. His painting thus belongs to the history of French art. In fact, his works rank among the most rare and beautiful of early French Romanticism: rare because Bonington died just days before his twenty-sixth birthday; beautiful because of the immediacy of his vision, the freshness of his color, and the confidence of his technique. These qualities are perfectly expressed in this small view near Rouen, which was painted outdoors, from an island in the midst of the Seine. It was probably made in the summer of 1825 while Bonington, who had already earned a medal at the previous year's Salon, was sharing a studio in Paris with Eugène Delacroix. Bonington's death in 1828 was mourned by a generation of French painters, including Delacroix, Théodore Rousseau, and Camille Corot, for whom Bonington was a conduit of the English notion of naturalistic and painterly landscape.

This picture was purchased from the direct descendant of its first owner; it is impeccably preserved and still has its original frame.

GT

century and the glamorous Hortense, who was a niece of Cardinal Mazarin. The plaster model for this bust is not among the trove of those by Dantan in the Musée Carnavalet, Paris.

JDD

Pierre-Jean David d'Angers
French, 1788–1856
Jeremy Bentham
Modeled ca. 1830; cast by Richard Eck et Durand before 1844
Bronze
Diam. 6¾ in. (17.1 cm)
Gift of Joseph G. Reinis, 2000
2000.455.2

The French Romantic sculptor David d'Angers was as fascinated by phrenology as Dantan was (see below left), but he disdained caricature. He modeled 454 identifiable portrait medallions, all with a sweeping earnestness in keeping with their subjects' greatness. They recall a period in Europe remarkable for its internationalism, including, as they do, spirits as diverse as Goethe, James Fenimore Cooper, and here the venerable English jurist and philosopher Jeremy Bentham (1748–1832), who was much admired in France. The donor is the author of the standard work *The Portrait Medallions of David d'Angers* (New York, 1999).

JDD

Jean-Pierre Dantan
French, 1800–1869
Bust of a Young Woman
Signed and dated 1836
Marble
H. (including base) 29½ in. (74.9 cm)
Gift of Michael Hall, in memory of W. R. Valentiner, 2000
2000.630.2

Dantan mixed Neoclassical training with interests in caricature, phrenology, and fashionable society. Today he is best known as a caricaturist, although straightforward portraits comprise at least half of his output. Occasionally, they may have a mischievous undertone, but this young woman has an appreciable semblance of wit and sparkle, even as she flaunts the latest coiffure. Dubbed "à la Hortense Mancini," the style was viewed as revivalistic, harking back to the seventeenth

Conrad Graf
Austrian, 1782–1851
Fortepiano
Vienna, 1838
Walnut veneer, various woods, iron and brass strings, leather, and cloth
L. 93¼ in. (236.8 cm)
Purchase, Amati Gifts, in memory of Frederick P. Rose, 2001
2001.272

One of the preeminent fortepiano makers of his day, Conrad Graf was the recipient of a gold medal at the 1835 Austrian Industrial Products Exhibition. His instruments were owned and played by leading pianists and composers, including Beethoven, Czerny, Schubert, Schumann, Kalkbrenner, Mendelssohn, Chopin, Liszt, and Brahms, as well as by such notables as the archduke and archduchess of Austria, the empress of Russia, the queen of Saxony, and the poet Goethe.

The nameplate of this fortepiano reads "CONRAD GRAF / kaiserl : kön : hof-forte-pianomacher / Wien / nächst der Carls-Kirche im Mondschein Nº. 102." Graf worked at that address from 1826 until his retirement in 1842.

The six-and-one-half-octave instrument features a Viennese action, which provides a light, shallow touch and enables the player to execute runs and ornaments with great facility. The stringing is considerably thinner and under less tension than that in the modern piano; this provides less volume but a brighter timbre, which in its day was likened to that of a fine wind instrument. The case is constructed almost entirely of wood (there is no metal frame, as in the modern piano). There are four pedals controlling the dampers, two moderators, and a keyboard shift.

SSP

Henri Chapu
French, 1833–1891
Music
Ca. 1869
Terracotta
Diam. 12⅝ in. (32 cm)
Inscribed: au docteur Delechamps; *signed:* Chapu
Purchase, Mrs. Sid R. Bass Gift, in honor of Mrs. Charles Wrightsman, and Rogers Fund, 2001
2001.4

Chapu was a Second Empire sculptor with rare lyric gifts. His young winged genius bows the violin before a cityscape that represents Thebes, the walls of which were said to have been raised to the strains of a lyre played by Amphion, the diminutive figure seated at right. The imagery thus unites the harmonies of music and architecture. This terracotta is the model for one of six silvered-bronze reliefs, allegories of the arts, that were destined for the drawing room of a house built by Chapu's architect friend Paul Sédille. Located in Paris on the boulevard Magenta, it was completed in 1870.

JDD

necessary, in favor of an imposing effect . . . [and] poetic charm." This photograph of a street in Nègre's hometown combines the broad patches of light and dark characteristic of early paper-negative photographs with a rigorously geometric structure; the whole composition is enlivened by carefully placed details, such as the young man seated on the hillside—somewhat improbably—as if leaning against the left edge of the picture.

MD

Jean-Baptiste Carpeaux
French, 1827–1875
Pietà
Ca. 1864
Terracotta
H. 11½ in. (29.1 cm)
Bearing the wax seal of the atelier
Purchase, Assunta Sommella Peluso, Ada Peluso, and Romano I. Peluso Gift, in memory of Ignazio Peluso, 2001
2001.199

Charles Nègre
French, 1820–1880
A Street in Grasse
1852
Salted paper print from paper negative
13 × 9⅜ in. (32.9 × 23.8 cm)
Purchase, Jennifer and Joseph Duke Gift and several members of The Chairman's Council Gifts, 2000
2000.286

Born in the Provençal town of Grasse in 1820, Nègre moved to Paris at nineteen to study painting in the studio of Paul Delaroche and arrived in the capital just a few months after the public announcement of the invention of photography. He began making daguerreotypes in the mid-1840s, but only with the ascendancy of paper negatives and prints around 1850 did he fully embrace photography, first as an aid to his painting and later as documentation and art.

After a photographic excursion to the south of France in August 1852, when this picture was made, Nègre wrote: "Being a painter myself, I have kept painters in mind. Wherever I could dispense with architectural precision I have indulged in the picturesque; in which case I have sacrificed a few details, when

Carpeaux demonstrates here an enduring admiration for the plangent heroism of Michelangelo, evinced earlier in the famous *Ugolino and His Sons,* conceived during his study years in Rome. (The marble, finished in 1867, is now owned by the Metropolitan Museum; acc. no. 67.250.) The government of Napoléon III kept Carpeaux busy with official projects, decorative sculpture, and portraiture, but it is clear from the evidence of the occasional private moments when he sketched sacred subjects, such as this group, that he would have been one of the most powerful of all religious artists had he been freer to exercise this repertory. Mounding the clay pellets and pressing them into shape in mere seconds, Carpeaux focused his entire attention upon the Virgin Mary's maternal embrace, to the virtual exclusion of Christ's legs. A related drawing in the Musée des Beaux-Arts, Valenciennes, is dated 1864.

JDD

Christopher Dresser (designer)
English, 1834–1904
Hukin and Heath (manufacturer)
English (Birmingham)
Traveling Tea Set
Ca. 1879
Gilt and silver-plated white metal (electroplate) and woven bamboo; case of leather-covered wood with velvet and glazed-cotton linings
H. (teakettle) 4⅜ in. (11.1 cm)
Partial and Promised Gift of an Anonymous Donor, in memory of Walter E. Stait, 2000
2000.594.1–.5

Although trained at the London School of Design, Dresser pursued a career in botany and obtained a Ph.D. from the University of Jena at twenty-six. Failing to become professor of botany at University College, London, he turned to designing mass-produced household wares, including carpets, silver, glass, furniture, metalwork, and wallpaper.

Dresser was impressed by the Japanese exhibits at the 1862 Paris Exposition Universelle and visited Japan in 1877. In his semiofficial capacity representing British manufacturers, he was accorded favored status to travel and to study decorative-arts production. His *Japan: Its Architecture, Art, and Art Manufactures* (London and New York, 1882) records his visit.

This tea set was designed after his return. The small pieces that fit inside the two large ones reflect the Japanese love of stacking boxes and conserving space. The woven bamboo on the handle is also Eastern in derivation. It is in his new interest in form, rather than pattern, that the influence of Dresser's Japanese experience is most noticeable. The shapes evoke ones readily encountered in Japan in wood or in a metal such as iron. The set was popular and produced in both sterling and electroplate for at least a decade.

JMcN

François Bonvin
French, 1817–1888
A Woman Spinning Wool
Charcoal on laid paper
15⅞ × 11⅝ in. (40.3 × 29.5 cm)
Signed and dated (lower left): f. Bonvin, 1861
Watermark: VanderLey *(with putto on sphere)*
Gift of Lila and Herman Shickman, 2000
2000.515

Bonvin believed art should express the truths of everyday life by including humble subjects and routine activities. Seeking to emphasize the simplicity and timelessness of what his sitters were doing, rather than who they were, he often portrayed women with their heads quietly bowed to domestic chores, such as knitting, grinding coffee, playing the piano, slicing bread, shucking oysters, or, as is seen here, twisting wool from a spindle into yarn.

By virtue of its subject, composition, technique, and size, our new drawing is now the most significant work by Bonvin in the Museum's collection, which also includes an early graphite work, a watercolor, and five etchings. The woman is one of four spinners drawn and etched by the artist between 1856 and 1861. An austere image, suffused with dusky, poetic light, it typifies Bonvin's best, mature work, which evolved from his study of seventeenth- and eighteenth-century painters, particularly Chardin.

CI

Henri Fantin-Latour

French, 1836–1904

Asters and Fruit on a Table

1868

Oil on canvas

22 ⅜ × 21 ⅝ in. (56.8 × 54.9 cm)

**The Walter H. and Leonore Annenberg
Collection, Partial Gift of Walter H. and
Leonore Annenberg, 2001**

2001.202.3

Writing in 1863, the critic Zachary Astruc praised Fantin-Latour's flower paintings as "marvels of color and artistic sensibility . . . as compelling as they are charming. They are tonal rhythms, freshness, abandon, surprising vivacity." Such qualities are handsomely exemplified in this picture, painted five years later. Fantin-Latour's reliance on a simple compositional scheme—in his own words, "flowers in the middle and fruit around them"—proved a successful strategy. Here a vase of China asters, placed on the vertical axis and flanked by a plate of grapes and a grouping of autumn fruits, serves as a foil for the play of resonant color and inventive surface effects. An overall sense of vitality is created by the restless, animate quality of brushwork and by the application of paint in a spare, dry manner that makes use of the interstices between the strokes. By varying the texture and density of pigment, Fantin-Latour evoked the translucent quality of the vase, the veneer of the light-dappled mahogany tabletop, and the lushness of ripe fruit and freshly picked flowers. Moreover, by retaining the spirit of his *pochades* (quick studies from nature) and his moody, introspective self-portraits, Fantin-Latour succeeded in producing a still life of originality and distinction.   SAS

Henri Fantin-Latour
French, 1836–1904
Roses and Lilies
1888
Oil on canvas
23½ × 18 in. (59.7 × 45.7 cm)
The Walter H. and Leonore Annenberg Collection, Partial Gift of Walter H. and Leonore Annenberg, 2001
2001.202.4

The summer Fantin-Latour made *Roses and Lilies* he claimed to be "very tired" of painting flowers. The admission is not surprising for an artist who had spent the previous thirty years producing still lifes expressly for an English market, but it is difficult to reconcile with the present work, originally owned by Fantin-Latour's patron and dealer, Ruth Edwards. One would be hard-pressed to find signs of fatigue or slackening of artistic sensibility in this splendid arrangement, deftly painted with sprightly flourishes of color, ranging from unexpected highlights of blue to creamy whites faintly dusted with mauve

and yellow. Fantin-Latour's signature roses, in full bloom in a rounded bowl, serve as a perfect counterpoint to the long, graceful stems of white lilies in a tall glass vase. Here, with unerring sensitivity, he perceived the nature of flowers "not with the enlarging lens" of the botanist—to quote James McNeill Whistler—"but the light of one who sees in the choice selection of brilliant tones and delicate tints future harmonies." At age fifty-two Fantin-Latour admirably met the challenge prescribed by the American artist three years earlier in his famous "Ten O'Clock" lecture.

SAS

Claude Monet
French, 1840–1926
Poppy Field, Argenteuil
1875
Oil on canvas
21¼ × 29 in. (54 × 73.7 cm)
The Walter H. and Leonore Annenberg
Collection, Partial Gift of Walter H. and
Leonore Annenberg, 2001
2001.202.5

The year 1875 marked a difficult moment for Monet. Sales of his work, and thus his income, were down significantly from the preceding years. The group of friends who had organized the first Impressionist exhibition of 1874 could not agree on the terms of a second exhibition, and the March 1875 auction that was held instead produced poor prices. Yet Monet pressed forward, continuing to paint pictures remarkable for their calm beauty and intimation of life unencumbered by worry. In his views of Argenteuil days are always sunny, poppies bloom continuously, children cavort freely, and ladies have nothing more pressing to do than to stroll with their parasols. In this respect his work of

the mid-1870s resembles that of Camille Corot, who died in February 1875. Like Corot at Ville-d'Avray, Monet chose motifs close to home—and improved on them.

This beautiful, archetypal Impressionist landscape betrays neither Monet's personal concerns nor those of the town of Argenteuil. Little could the viewer have realized that the plain of Gennevilliers, depicted here, had become a dumping ground for Parisian effluent. We must recognize, then, that Monet's painting was an act of consolation (for himself) and reassurance (for his prospective patrons) that nature and simple pleasures would endure.

GT

Hilaire-Germain-Edgar Degas
French, 1834–1917
Dancer
Ca. 1880
Pastel, charcoal, and chalk on paper
19¼ × 12½ in. (48.9 × 31.8 cm)
The Walter H. and Leonore Annenberg
Collection, Partial Gift of Walter H. and
Leonore Annenberg, 2001
2001.202.2

Degas frequently drew from models, and some of the dancers who posed for him, such as Nelly Franklin and Marie van Goethem, are now better known for that role than for their dancing skills. However, Degas transformed these real dancers into a fictive ballet troupe that rehearsed constantly in his imagination and performed only in his pictures.

For this fine pastel Degas selected a gesture—the adjustment of a sash and skirt—that he had included in a number of pictures and made it the central event in a new work. Although he had doubtless observed dancers adjusting their costumes during his visits to the *foyer de la danse,* it is unlikely that he had ever seen this particular scene in a rehearsal. Dancers did not wear sashes—or neck ribbons, for that matter—during practice, and only rarely on stage. But the sashes were crucial to Degas because they enabled him to bring bright splashes of color to a scene that would otherwise have tended toward the drab. This pastel, then, is not a study from life, although a model may have posed for the artist. Instead, it is a completely artificial, and artfully convincing, representation: a slice of art rather than a slice of life.

GT

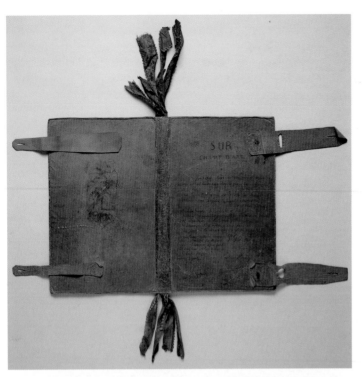

Paul Gauguin
French, 1848–1903
The Artist's Portfolio, Pont-Aven
1894
Watercolor and gouache over charcoal, on heavy gray wove (blotting) paper, mounted to inside covers; leather binding inscribed in pen and ink with additions in watercolor; multicolored silk ribbons stitched into binding
Each drawing 16 ¾ × 10 ⅜ in. (42.5 × 26.4 cm)
Signed in brush and wash (left-hand drawing, lower left): PGO 94
Promised Gift of Leon D. and Debra R. Black, and Purchase, Joseph Pulitzer and Florence B. Selden Bequests, and 1999 Benefit Fund, 2000

2000.255

When Gauguin returned to France after his first trip to Tahiti, he headed to the picturesque village of Pont-Aven, on the Breton coast, in the hope of recapturing the exhilaration he had experienced while painting there in previous years. Unfortunately, on this visit his activity was restricted by a fractured leg he suffered in a brawl with sailors. Thus, instead of standing before his easel, the artist spent much of his time seated, creating works on paper, many of which are likely to have been stored in this portfolio. The watercolors he drew on its inside covers, probably during the summer of 1894, recall subjects Gauguin had treated before in Brittany: the rolling landscape, serpentine waterways, and simple products of country life.

The mock-heroic presentation of this portfolio to the safekeeping of the innkeeper Marie-Jeanne Gloanec—as formally set forth in writing on its front cover—may have constituted the grand finale to a bibulous evening Gauguin spent with his artist cronies Roderic O'Conor, Eric Forbes-Robertson, and Armand Séguin, whose names are inscribed in the dedication. This extraordinary work, surely one of Gauguin's most appealing excursions into the decorative arts, remained virtually unknown until recently.

CI

Hilaire-Germain-Edgar Degas
French, 1834–1917
**Paule Gobillard, Jeannie Gobillard,
Julie Manet, and Geneviève Mallarmé**
December 16, 1895
Gelatin silver print
11⅛ × 15¼ in. (28.4 × 38.9 cm)
Gift of Paul F. Walter, 2000
2000.655.1

After making the majority of his paintings and experimenting with pastel and monotype, Degas briefly turned to photography in late 1895. Friends described him as "ablaze with enthusiasm" as he enlisted them as models and appropriated their living rooms as his after-dinner photographic studio. Both the activity and the resulting images bound Degas to his circle of close friends and brought comfort in the evening hours, when he otherwise dwelled on his own mortality and the recent deaths of his brother Achille and sister Marguerite.

One December evening, in the company of Auguste Renoir and Stéphane Mallarmé, Degas photographed Mallarmé's daughter Geneviève and "the little Manet girls"—Julie Manet (the seventeen-year-old daughter of Berthe Morisot and Édouard Manet's brother Eugène) and her cousins Paule and Jeannie Gobillard, all three of them orphans whom the elder artists had taken under their wing. Sitting before Degas, whose camera is reflected in the mirror, the young women are joined to one another by the continuous blackness of their dresses, a backdrop for the gentle rhythm of their hands.

Degas never exhibited his photographs publicly, preferring instead to keep them a part of the private realm in which they were made; he gave this tender picture to Julie Manet.

MD

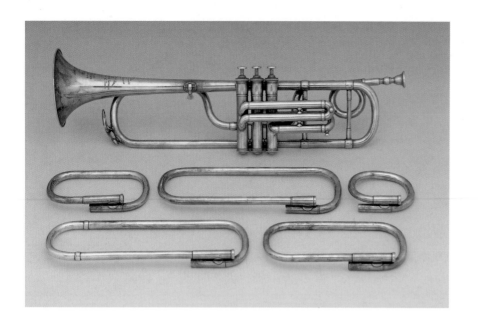

Émile Decoeur
French, 1876–1953
Edmond Lachenal
French, 1855–1948
Vase
Châtillon-sous-Bagneux, ca. 1900–1905
Glazed stoneware
H. 10¾ in. (27.3 cm)
**The Charles E. Sampson Memorial Fund,
2001**
2001.92

Stoneware was the preferred medium for
many ceramic artists working in France in
the decades around 1900. It is more durable
than earthenware and easier to form than
porcelain, which is far less pliable. Further-
more, the temperatures at which stoneware
is fired allow for spectacular glazing effects.
Edmond Lachenal and his pupil Émile Decoeur
were two of the many French ceramicists who
learned to exploit the somewhat random and
unpredictable qualities of stoneware glazes,
which can produce highly mottled surfaces with
pronounced variations in color and texture.

The complex and seemingly uncontrolled
aspects of many of these glazes made them
particularly appropriate for vessels in the Art
Nouveau style, such as this example, in
which naturalistic forms and asymmetries
often prevailed. In this vase, probably by

Courtois and Mille
French (Paris), 1880–98
Valve Trumpet
Ca. 1881–85
Silver-plated brass; original wood case
L. 20½ in. (52.1 cm)
**Purchase, Bequest of Robert Alonzo
Lehman, by exchange, 2001**
2001.187a–i

Antoine Courtois fils (active 1844–80) was
one of the leading Paris manufacturers of
cornets à pistons and orchestral trumpets.
After 1880, when Auguste Mille (1838–1898)
took over the workshop of about twenty-five
employees, the company maintained its
high reputation. This so-called low trumpet,
pitched in F with exchangeable terminal
crooks for the keys E, E-flat, D, C, and B-
flat (A), is equipped with Périnet valves. It
is a fine, typical example of a French trumpet
of the period 1860 to 1920. This instrument
is the type on which students were taught at
the Paris conservatory and that was played in
French orchestras of the era between Bizet
(d. 1875) and Debussy (d. 1918). About 1920
the high B-flat trumpet, already in use in
other countries, replaced this type in France.
As the engraving on the bell indicates, the
trumpet came to the United States through
the company's American agent, John Howard
Foote, in New York. It was not used very
much, probably because in the United States
the B-flat trumpet had already replaced the
low trumpet by about 1900.   HH

Decoeur, the organic quality imparted by the sinuous, tendril-like handles is reinforced by the richly mottled glaze, in which purples merge into grays of varying intensity. Despite the subtle sculptural quality of the vase, the glaze rather than the form creates the primary aesthetic impact.   JHM

Édouard Vuillard
French, 1868–1940
Album
1895
Oil on canvas
26¾ × 80½ in. (67.9 × 204.5 cm)
The Walter H. and Leonore Annenberg Collection, Partial Gift of Walter H. and Leonore Annenberg, 2000
2000.93.2

In 1895 Thadée and Misia Natanson commissioned from Vuillard a series of five decorative panels. Collectively known as *Album,* they took the title of the largest of the paintings, in which a portfolio or album is the center of attention.

Languid women suspended in sumptuous, flower-filled interiors are the subject of all five paintings, which are of various sizes. Figures and objects blend in a profusion of patterns, and their closely ranged tonalities of earthy browns, burgundies, and yellows evoke tapestries.

The panels' unusual character matched that of the Natansons' apartment on rue Saint-Florentin, just off the place de la Concorde, which consisted of a large open space adjoined by several small alcove areas. Its unconventional decor reflected Misia's taste, which was inspired by the English Arts and Crafts movement. Also called the "Annex," the apartment often served as an alternative office for the artists and writers who contributed to Thadée's lively avant-garde journal, *La revue blanche;* among them were Claude Debussy, Léon Blum, Stéphane Mallarmé, and André Gide. The evocative Symbolist qualities of Mallarmé's poetry and Debussy's music also find echoes in Vuillard's five panels.   SR

Masonic Armchair

American (Boston, Massachusetts), 1760–75
Mahogany, maple, gilding, and horsehair
H. 50½ in. (128.3 cm)

**Gift of Mr. and Mrs. George M. Kaufman,
2000**

2000.192

A magnificent exception to the rule that all eighteenth-century American furniture conforms to standard models is this great Masonic armchair from Boston. Such ceremonial chairs, of richly carved Rococo design, were all the rage for the masters and wardens of Masonic lodges in the provincial cities of mid-eighteenth-century England. However, none is known from Philadelphia, the center of Rococo fashion in America, and but one—our new acquisition—from all of New England.

The chair, twelve inches taller than normal, is monumental. Its back is composed of Masonic symbols: fluted columns (King Solomon's temple), rusticated arch (arch of heaven), compass and square (faith and reason), mason's level (equality), serpent swallowing its tail (rebirth), and trowel (cement of brotherly love). Its legs—with brilliantly executed flat-carved, acanthus-leaf knees and

raked-back talon-ball feet—are characteristic of Boston, but the lodge for which it was made remains a mystery.

This impressive icon of Freemasonry and colonial woodwork is remarkably well preserved. The mahogany's undisturbed finish has deep red, luminous highlights, and the gilding on the feet is original (some of the other gold was added later, probably in 1790, the year painted on the back of the splat). The striped horsehair seat covering, though Neoclassical in style, also appears to be original.

MHH

Gilbert Stuart
American, 1755–1828
Captain John Gell
1785
Oil on canvas
94½ × 58½ in. (240 × 148.6 cm)
Purchase, Dorothy Schwartz Gift, Joseph Pulitzer Bequest, and 2000 Benefit Fund, 2000
2000.450

In his long and prolific career Gilbert Stuart painted only seven full-length portraits (other than those of George Washington). His ambitious and imposing likeness of Captain John Gell (1738–1806) is the second in this series. Stuart executed it in London and there looked to Sir Joshua Reynolds for advice on blending ideal and individual characteristics in grand portraiture. The image epitomizes Stuart's adaptation of Reynolds's manner: The picture is an accomplished combination of fine and apparently slapdash brushwork that conveys an image of heroism and naturalism, duty and sensibility. It suggests spontaneity in execution, belying Stuart's considerable conceptual strategy and technical facility.

In 1785 Gell had just completed his duty on the *Monarca,* a seventy-gun ship that he had commanded in a series of five naval engagements against the French. He came from a Derbyshire family and was made a lieutenant in the Royal Navy in 1760. Two years later he was promoted to commander, a rank he held for thirty years through active duty in Nova Scotia, the East Indies, Portugal, Toulon, and Genoa, among other places. He advanced to the rank of admiral in 1799.

CRB

François M. Guyol de Guiran
French, active in America 1812–28
Portrait of a Gentleman and His Daughter
1800–1825
Watercolor on ivory and painted paper
W. (including frame) 6⅛ in. (15.6 cm)
Purchase, Gift of The Chester Dale Collection, by exchange, 2001
2001.95

Guyol de Guiran is known exclusively by this signed piece, a work of striking quality and originality. The artist was one of the many French-émigré miniaturists who came to America in the early nineteenth century, when the market was especially strong for such delicate likenesses. The Museum's collection of works by these painters is extensive and greatly enhanced by this touchstone portrait. Guyol de Guiran worked in St. Louis (1812–ca. 1820) and in New Orleans (1822–28); this picture may have been done in either locale. It is presumably a portrayal of a father and daughter, given the age difference and the loving glance from the girl to her gentleman companion, but this relationship cannot be confirmed. An unusual feature of the tiny painting is the artist's joining of ivory, on which the figures are delineated, with paper, on which the foliage is drawn.   CRB

Miss Leland
American
Boy with Pull Toy
Ca. 1825
Watercolor on ivory
4¼ × 4 in. (10.8 × 10.2 cm)
Purchase, Martha Fleischman Gift, in honor of her mother, Barbara G. Fleischman, 2000
2000.484

The Museum's collection of American portrait miniatures has become increasingly comprehensive with the addition of fine works by heretofore unknown miniaturists, such as this enchanting portrait of a beautifully dressed boy with his pull-toy horse. The obscure but obviously talented Miss Leland signed and dated the work on the original backing paper for the ivory, and it may be that this inscribed example will lead to the discovery of other pieces by the artist. All too often, miniatures of children served a memorial function, but this piece, by contrast, appears to be a life-affirming image.

                    CRB

Boston and Sandwich Glass Company, New England Glass Company, or South Boston Flint Glass Works
American, 1825–88; 1818–88; 1819–?70
Cream Pitcher and Sugar Bowl
Sandwich, East Cambridge, or South Boston, Massachusetts, 1820–35
Blown lead glass
H. (pitcher) 6⅛ in. (15.4 cm); h. (bowl with lid) 9⅞ in. (25.1 cm)
Gift of Mr. and Mrs. Robert Keller, in memory of Gretchen Keller, 2000
2000.509.1; .2a, b

Glass, elaborately cut or engraved in a variety of patterns based on English Regency styles, was in vogue for fine tableware during the early nineteenth century. This elegant cream pitcher and sugar bowl reveal a sophisticated alternative to cutting: the manipulation of the clear, colorless glass in its molten state. The vessels combine multiple decorative techniques characteristic of three New England factories that were producing stylish wares during the 1820s and 1830s. The predominant feature is the tooled horizontal ribbing on a second gather, or applied layer, of glass, which was drawn upward into the ribs with a sharp tool to create a swag pattern. This striking ornamentation is repeated on the domed cover of the sugar bowl and again on the cover's finial. The bold, classic footed shapes and the rounded hollow stems are hallmarks of all three Massachusetts firms. Although lacking the refractive qualities of their cut-glass counterparts, the cream pitcher and sugar bowl are highly lustrous in their surfaces and sophisticated in their decorative techniques.

ACF

J. and I. Cox (designer, manufacturer, and/or retailer)
American, 1818–52
Lamp
New York City and/or England, ca. 1825
Gilt bronze and brass, with blown-glass half-dome shade
H. 28 in. (71.1 cm)
Purchase, Dr. and Mrs. Burton P. Fabricand, Mrs. Daniel Fraad, and Jan and Warren Adelson Gifts, 2000
2000.449

"Sinumbra" lamps, so named because they were designed to reduce the shadow cast by traditional Argand lamps, enjoyed great popularity in fashionable American interiors during the 1820s and 1830s. This elegant example is distinguished by a rare label of J. and I. Cox (for John and Joseph), leading New York City purveyors of lighting fixtures. By touting the firm's role as "maker," when many of the lamps Cox marked are known to have been produced in England, the label suggests a different role: Cox may have assembled the lamp entirely from imported parts or made some of the elements itself.

The painted glass shade is a rare survival and would have been used on lamps of this type; however, it is not known whether this one is original to the lamp. The scenes resemble British aquatints and are similar to drawings by John Hill, a British-born artist who emigrated to New York City. They also resemble the work of William Collins, an English enameler and manufacturer of glass. This example is among the finest surviving glass shades of the early nineteenth century.

MH

William Trost Richards
American, 1833–1905
Lago Avernus
Ca. 1867–70
Watercolor, gouache, and graphite on blue-gray laid paper
4½ × 9½ in. (11.4 × 24.1 cm)
Morris K. Jesup Fund, 2001
2001.39

Probably executed on Richards's second trip to Europe in 1866–67, *Lago Avernus* is one of a handful of his early landscapes in watercolor. His interest in this medium was undoubtedly stimulated by the founding, at the time of his departure, of the American Society of Painters in Water Color, which would provide a forum for him and for many other American artists. In England Richards saw the watercolors of J. M. W. Turner, whose influence is conspicuous here in the subject (the volcanic lake near Naples that Turner had painted several times), the composition, and the mixture of transparent and opaque pigments, as well as in a textured blue paper very similar to that often used by Turner.

Lago Avernus may be the model for Richards's unlocated watercolor *Lake Avernus,* his first submission to the society, in 1870. In the same year he met Reverend Elias Lyman Magoon, who purchased many of the artist's watercolors of American scenery and gave them to the Metropolitan in 1880. The acquisition of *Lago Avernus* adds to our rich collection of the artist's work in various media, begun more than a century ago and enhanced particularly during the last decade.

KJA

Lyon and Healy
American (Chicago, Illinois), est. 1864
Pedal Harp
Ca. 1895
Wood, ebonized and gilt; brass; and iron
H. 70 in. (177.8 cm)
Purchase, Clara Mertens Bequest, in memory of André Mertens, 2001
2001.171

In 1889 Lyon and Healy, a successful retail and mail-order musical merchandising company, added the manufacture of harps to its business. Within a decade the firm became a serious international competitor and soon surpassed the Paris companies of Erard and Pleyel. Lyon and Healy's success was built on sturdy and durable wooden construction and smooth and secure action of the metal rods and levers, which were crafted with the highest precision. The basic construction, however, follows the French models, in particular Erard's double-action harp.

The present example, with the serial number 115, is among the company's earliest to survive. It corresponds to model number 23 in Lyon and Healy's first trade catalogue for harps, which appeared about 1900. The instrument is a semigrand harp, with seven double-action pedals and an eighth pedal for a swell mechanism to increase the volume. It also features a fourchette mechanism, which

terminates the sounding length of the forty-five strings, and a semicircular body. Body base, column, and harmonic bar are ebonized and richly decorated with gilt flowers, birds, and a human figure.   HH

James McNeill Whistler
American, 1834–1903
Variations in Violet and Gray—Market Place, Dieppe
1885
Watercolor and gouache on off-white wove paper
8 × 5 in. (20.2 × 12.7 cm)
Gift of Douglass Campbell, Richard Strachan, and Stephen M. Strachan, in memory of Mrs. Douglass Campbell and Mrs. William Lyman Campbell, 2000
2000.512

During Whistler's visit in 1885 to the Normandy seaside resort of Dieppe, he captured the busy market square from a high vantage point and accentuated the liveliness of the scene by using his sheet in a vertical format. The result was one of his most delightful and complex watercolors, filled with energy, variety, and interest despite its surprisingly small size. The sheet offers a catalogue of the techniques Whistler had mastered by the mid-1880s, the zenith of his work in watercolor. Precise brushstrokes create picturesque figures gathered in the foreground, abstract dabs suggest the distant crowd, and delicate washes indicate old buildings around the square. The title, *Variations in Violet and Gray,* invokes both the musical associations that Whistler so often pursued in creating and naming his works and his preference for harmonious arrangements distilled from the world of appearances.

Following the successful London exhibition of the watercolor in 1886, it was shown in Paris in 1887, to acclaim and appreciation by contemporaries such as Camille Pissarro, and in New York in 1889. Its rich exhibition history enhances its importance, which Whistler himself appears to have recognized.

HBW

THE FALES COLLECTION OF AMERICAN JEWELRY

Clockwise, from top left

Pair of Earrings with Snap-On Covers

American, ca. 1882–85
Diamonds, gold, and enamel
L. (each earring) ⅞ in. (2.2 cm);
diam. (each cover) ½ in. (1.3 cm)

Locket

American (Boston, Massachusetts), 1706
Gold, crystal, and hair
L. 1 in. (2.5 cm)

Tiffany and Company

American, est. 1837
Pin
New York City, ca. 1890
Gold, enamel, and diamond
L. 3¼ in. (8.3 cm)

George W. Jamison

American, d. 1868
Cameo
New York City, ca. 1835
Helmet-conch shell, enamel, and yellow, rose,
and green gold
L. 2½ in. (6.4 cm)

Marcus and Company

American, 1892–before 1950
Brooch
New York City, ca. 1900
Gold, peridot, diamonds, pearls, and enamel
L. 2½ in. (6.4 cm)

Purchase, Susan and Jon Rotenstreich Gift, 2001

2001.234a–d; 2000.532; 2001.330; 2000.562;
2001.238

The Museum recently purchased an important collection of American jewelry made between 1706 and 1915. This comprehensive group of seventy-three objects and sets includes several exceptional examples of the jeweler's art, including those pictured here. The heart-shaped locket with light brown hair beneath a faceted crystal is the earliest piece in the collection. A type of mourning jewelry, it is inscribed "ob^t 20 / of April / 1706" above an engraved skull. The helmet-conch-shell cameo with a bust of Andrew Jackson, cut in about 1835 by George W. Jamison, is an elegant tribute to the seventh president. Reflecting the "cameo fever" that first swept Europe in the late eighteenth century, it is inscribed with Jackson's oft-quoted slogan, THE UNION / IT MUST AND / SHALL BE / PRESERVED. Beauty and practicality are combined in the diamond-drop earrings with removable "coach" covers, which served to protect and conceal the valuable stones. The boldly scrolled, gold-mounted peridot brooch with diamonds and a pendant pearl, marked by the outstanding New York firm of Marcus and Company, harks back to Renaissance designs. A diamond dewdrop shimmers amidst the realistically rendered enamel petals of a flower-form pin, one of several exquisite Tiffany and Company pieces in the Fales Collection.   BCW

Louis Comfort Tiffany
American, 1848–1933
Tiffany Glass and Decorating Company
Corona, New York, 1892–1902
Two Vases
Blown Favrile glass
H. (.1) 22 in. (55.9 cm); h. (.2) 16 ⅛ in. (41 cm)
Gift of Robert and Gladys Koch, 1999
1999.412.1, .2

The Metropolitan Museum has one of the most comprehensive and historically important collections of blown Favrile glass by Louis Comfort Tiffany. However, the gift of these two superb vases immeasurably enhances it. Both epitomize Tiffany's goal to produce one-of-a-kind works that expressed his personal aesthetic. Each has a coloration of gold with an iridescent surface, and yet each is treated in a markedly different way. The vase on the left is unusually large and is a prime example of Tiffany's passion for depicting nature. An arrangement of leaves and stems is displayed fluidly over the body.

The vase on the right exhibits entirely abstract decoration, achieved by the varying surfaces of crusty, deep chocolate brown (akin to those on Tiffany's Cypriote glasses) contrasted with smooth, rich iridescent gold; the overall design undulates in a manner that brings to mind the prevailing Art Nouveau style.

Like the Museum's other holdings of Favrile vessels (originally owned by Tiffany or by the H. O. Havemeyers), the larger of the two vases has a significant provenance. It was exhibited at the Paris Exposition Universelle of 1900 and was owned by Tiffany's sister, Mrs. Alfred Mitchell, of New Haven.

ACF

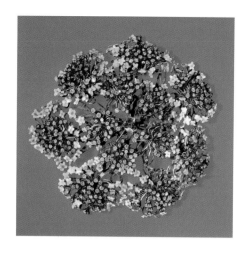

Louis Comfort Tiffany
American, 1848–1933
Hair Ornament
New York City, ca. 1904
Silver, copper, opals, demantoid garnets, garnets, and enamel
Diam. 3½ in. (8.9 cm)
Purchase, Barrie A. and Deedee Wigmore Gift, 2001
2001.249

Louis C. Tiffany, already a master of many media, began making jewelry shortly after 1900. While designers at his father's firm, Tiffany and Company, utilized primarily pearls, diamonds, and other precious stones, Louis's work was more closely aligned with that of the avant-garde Parisian jewelers René Lalique and Georges Fouquet, and, like them, he favored the common forms in nature as well as semiprecious stones and enamel. The opals, garnets, and enamel on this piece provide a subtle interplay of light and color. As is consistent with Tiffany's earliest handwrought designs—inspired by field flowers and fruits—this hair ornament is based on the wild carrot, or Queen Anne's lace.

Tiffany first exhibited his jewelry to the public in 1904 at the Louisiana Purchase Exposition in St. Louis. Three ornaments of Queen Anne's lace, each representing the blossom at a different stage, were among the twenty-seven works that he displayed. This example, with its slightly domed blossom head, was the one cited in the contemporary press as being in "the full perfection of bloom" and was considered the most brilliant of the three. It descended in the family of the original owner, Ida E. B. Noyes (Mrs. LaVerne Noyes, d. 1912), a noted Chicago philanthropist, who probably purchased it at the 1904 fair.

ACF

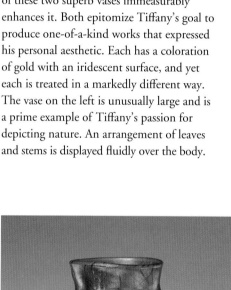

1999.412.1

1999.412.2

Paul Cézanne
French, 1839–1906
Still Life with a Watermelon and Pomegranates
1900–1906
Watercolor over graphite on heavy wove paper
12 × 18½ in. (30.5 × 47 cm)
The Walter H. and Leonore Annenberg Collection, Partial Gift of Walter H. and Leonore Annenberg, 2001
2001.202.1

Of the twenty or so still lifes Cézanne produced on paper during his final years, this watercolor is among the most fully realized. The composition is crowded with rotund fruit and tableware and colored intensely with a complete rainbow of hues, from the deep blue of the watermelon to the blazing red of the pomegranates (in French, *grenades*).

In another watercolor done at the same "sitting" Cézanne studied the same arrangement of objects but moved his position a quarter turn around the table. His second take (now in a private collection in Switzerland) shows the glass carafe—seen in this work at far right—in the center foreground of the composition; the wine bottle, with its paper label gleaming here above the melon, there stands behind the sugar bowl. The artist's shifted viewpoint altered entirely the regiment of forms he had at first admired, but presented a new "objectscape" to engage his love of shapes and spaces.

Of the nine watercolors by Cézanne now in the Museum's collection, this is our first still life.   CI

Claude Monet

French, 1840–1926

The Path through the Irises

1914–17

Oil on canvas

78⅞ × 70⅞ in. (200.3 × 180 cm)

The Walter H. and Leonore Annenberg Collection, Partial Gift of Walter H. and Leonore Annenberg, 2001

2001.202.6

Monet devoted the last dozen years of his life to the extraordinary large-scale decorative cycle that was installed in the Orangerie, Paris, after his death. With only a handful of exceptions, the motifs for the two hundred canvases on which he worked after his 1908 trip to Venice were taken from the extensive gardens that he had developed on his property at Giverny, and these canvases all relate in one way or another to the Orangerie cycle. His views of the water-lily pond are perhaps the most famous, but he also worked hard to extract novel compositions from other corners of his garden, where there were diverse plantings such as weeping willows, roses, and irises.

Like those he made of water lilies, his paintings of irises were meant to rise from the particular to the universal. In this work, the most highly finished of the series, the flowers are offered not as botanical specimens but as archetypes. Monet focused his energies on the movement of the swordlike leaves and on the unusual harmony of ocher, violet, blue green, and yellow green. Although the artist was already experiencing great difficulties with his eyesight, any grower of irises will recognize that he knowingly found the reddish purple tint that hides within every blue iris.

GT

57

Henri Matisse
French, 1869–1954
Seated Nude Asleep
1906
Woodcut
Image 18¾ × 15 in. (47.6 × 38.1 cm)
Signed and numbered (lower right):
Henri–Matisse 38/50; *initialed (in the block, lower left):* hm
Purchase, Reba and Dave Williams Gift, 2000
2000.236

A proof of *Seated Nude Asleep* was shown in Paris at the Salon des Indépendants in 1907. Reviewing the exhibition, a friend of the artist complained of the work's "willful deformations, a bit too premeditated." More than forty years later the great Matisse scholar Alfred H. Barr praised this work as presenting a "figure more uncompromising in its distortions and angularities than *The Blue Nude* (1907)," the artist's boldest Fauve painting. Even today the printed image has lost little of its original impact.

This is the largest and best known of three woodcuts of reclining or seated nudes that Matisse created in 1906. These prints—his only attempts in the medium—are indeed black-on-white equivalents of his strongest Fauve pictures. Matisse did not attempt to invest the nude with sensuous appeal. Instead, he concentrated on simplification and design. The contorted body rests on a background that is also Fauve in its combination of dots, daubs, and straight and wavy lines.

Woodcut was in vogue among the artist's colleagues in France and Germany. While the latter gouged directly into the block, Matisse created studies for his prints. The ink drawing for this work was recently acquired by the Metropolitan as part of the Jacques and Natasha Gelman bequest (acc. no. 1999.363.39). The block is owned by the British Museum, London.   SR

Evening Wrap
French, 1918–20
Ivory silk georgette with seed-bead embroidery
L. (center back) 58 in. (147.3 cm)
Isabel Shults Fund, 2001
2001.374.1

Evening coats, wraps, and mantles of the 1910s were opportunities for lavish embellishment. Their draped, kimono-like construction, composed of large, relatively uncut lengths of fabric, often accommodated expansive fields of applied ornament in long continuous bands. In this dramatic example a motif of stylized roses popularized by the designs of Raoul Dufy for Paul Poiret, the preeminent couturier of his day, is rendered in black on a white ground. A contrasting wide band controlling the back hem and train is embellished with a white-on-white centered spray of roses in a similar style. The highly graphic patterning described in the densely applied beading is evidence not only of the bold and dramatic effects characteristic of the period, but also of the miraculous recovery of the French luxury trades after the horrific disruption of World War I.

Although this wrap is typical of the late 1910s in its essentially linear drape—the result of the weight of the beading on a sheer silk georgette ground—its cocoonlike embrace and severely pegged hem also evoke the exotic themes introduced by Serge Diaghilev's Ballets Russes, which had inspired Poiret's languid odalisque styles of a decade earlier.   HK

Henry Ossawa Tanner
American, 1859–1937
Flight into Egypt
1923
Oil on canvas
29 × 26 in. (73.7 × 66 cm)
Marguerite and Frank A. Cosgrove Jr.
Fund, 2001
2001.402

Tanner's eloquent *Flight into Egypt* is a
canonical mature work by the increasingly
esteemed American artist, who studied in
Paris and resided in France. In the mid-1890s
Tanner decided to concentrate on biblical
themes familiar from his childhood in a
household headed by a leader of the African
Methodist Episcopal Church. Tanner developed an increasingly painterly, highly personal style based on empirical observation
and inner vision. "Tanner blues," complex
layers of glazes, and flat decorative surfaces
are keynotes of many of his late canvases.

Flight into Egypt depicts the Holy Family's
clandestine evasion of King Herod's assassins
(Matthew 2:12–14), Tanner's favorite biblical
story. It expresses his sensitivity to issues of
personal freedom, escape from persecution,
and migrations of African-Americans from
the South to the North. The painting, which
reveals a concern for human emotions and
an awareness of the mystical meanings of
biblical narratives, also manifests Tanner's
affiliation with contemporary Symbolism and
the religious revival that occurred in response
to challenges of the modern era.

On the back of this canvas is a study for
the prizewinning work Tanner entitled *Christ
at the Home of Lazarus,* painted about 1912
and now known only from photographs.

HBW

Otto Dix
German, 1891–1969
Nelly
1924
Lithograph
11⅛ × 8 in. (28.3 × 20.3 cm)
Signed (in the stone, lower right): DIX24
Purchase, Reba and Dave Williams Gift,
2000
2000.112.2

During the 1920s the painter and printmaker
Otto Dix was prominent in the German
art movement known as *Neue Sachlichkeit*
(New Objectivity). This portrait study is a
fine example of his emulation of the drafts-
manship of Northern Renaissance artists.

Nelly is a small lithograph of the artist's
daughter (1923–1955) at age one. She is shown
in Dix's customary close-up, three-quarter
view, which accentuates the roundness of her
full face. Her curly hair is a tousled mop, and
she wears an elaborate lace collar, which fits
tightly around her chubby neck. The portrait
conveys vitality and a nascent personality,
although not endearment. Nelly stares deter-
minedly ahead, and her purposeful mouth
suggests an intensity of character, even at
such a young age. Dix's dedication to un-
sparing, clinical objectivity extended even
to his depiction of his own young daughter.
He portrayed her with not many traces of
paternal sentiment.

This print is a welcome addition to the
Museum's holdings of works by modern
German artists such as Dix and Max Beckmann
(1884–1950), an area of collecting that has been
made possible by Reba and Dave Williams.

ALS

Josef Hoffmann
Austrian, 1870–1956
Tea Service
Silver, ebony, amethyst, and carnelian
H. (large teapot) 5 ⅜ in. (13.7 cm)
Cynthia Hazen Polsky and Leon B. Polsky Fund, 2000
2000.278.1–.9

Josef Hoffmann's designs before 1900 incorporated the curvilinear, organic motifs common to the then-fashionable Jugendstil and Art Nouveau styles. With the turn of the century, however, he abruptly abandoned them for a revolutionary new approach based on geometry, of which this tea service is an outstanding example. Its materials are lavish: hand-beaten silver, ebony, and semiprecious stones. Hoffmann, however, has integrated them with forms of uncompromising austerity: straight sides, domed lids, and squared-off handles. The only decoration, except for the inset jewels, is the single thin horizontal line of raised dots near the bottom of each container.

This service was made for the Wiener Werkstatte, the company of designers, artists, and craftsmen founded in Vienna in 1903 to produce luxury objects in the most advanced style. The set was purchased in 1911 by a San Francisco couple on their European wedding journey and descended from them to their grandson, the vendor to the Museum.

JSJ

Jacques Le Chevallier
French, 1896–1987
Lamp
Ca. 1928
Aluminum and ebonite
H. 11 in. (27.9 cm)
Purchase, The Horace W. Goldsmith Foundation Gift, 2001
2001.410a, b

Although most prolific as an artist in stained glass, Jacques Le Chevallier is perhaps best known for the small number of extraordinary Modernist table lamps that he designed in the late 1920s. This model, the most extreme of the group, consists of an abstract sculptural housing for the bulb resting atop a circular base raised on cylindrical legs. Starkly spare and completely unornamented, the lamp gives the overall effect of a functional machine. Nonetheless, a certain decorative quality is achieved through the Cubist-inspired angular planes, the exposed screws and braces, and the softly reflective finish. No effort has been made to conceal the bulb or the socket, though the light can be shaded or redirected by revolving the lamp to a variety of different positions. Less reflective than silver or chrome-plated steel, aluminum was more affordable during the 1920s, increasing its appeal for designers.

Le Chevallier was a founding member of the Union des Artistes Modernes, an organization that promoted the forward-looking, reform-minded ideals of Modernist design in France. Other members included architects and designers such as Pierre Chareau, René Herbst, Eileen Gray, Robert Mallet-Stevens, and Charlotte Perriand.

JG

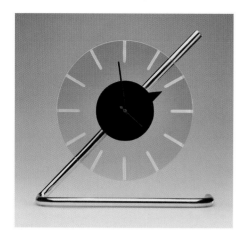

Gilbert Rohde
American, 1894–1944
Electric Clock
Ca. 1933
Chrome-plated metal and glass
H. 12⅛ in. (30.8 cm)
John C. Waddell Collection, Gift of
John C. Waddell, 2000
2000.600.15

Rohde was known primarily as a furniture maker whose progressive designs were produced by well-known manufacturers such as Heywood Wakefield, Troy Sunshade, John Widdicomb, Herman Miller, and Thonet. In 1932 and 1933 he created a series of clocks for the Herman Miller Clock Company that were remarkable for their daringly advanced designs. The transparent glass face of this example is suspended in front of a chromed diagonal support, its sharp angle abstractly reinforcing a sense of dynamic motion. The "numerals"—slashes of white—seem to float on the clear glass surface, highlighting the sharp, dominant black hour hand. The color scheme of black, red, and silver and the use of sleek materials such as chrome and glass typify the kind of furnishings that complemented luxury interiors of the 1930s. Although most people were struggling to make ends meet during the decade-long Great Depression, the elegant penthouse atop a skyscraper apartment building represented a privileged fantasy world that dominated Hollywood movie sets as well as designs for luxury city dwellings created by the most contemporary architects and designers.

JA

Terence Harold Robsjohn-Gibbings
American (b. England), 1905–1976
Klismos Chair
Ca. 1937
Wood and vellum
H. 35⅜ in. (89.9 cm)
Purchase, The Horace W. Goldsmith
Foundation Gift, 2001
2001.207

Although the 1930s saw an increasing acceptance of the aesthetics of Modernism, traditional design continued to be dominant. Most people found its references to a settled past reassuring. The styles of the eighteenth and early nineteenth centuries, more or less accurately copied, were especially popular. However, even Neoclassicism, which might be assumed to be the safest of styles, could be challenging if carried to extremes.

Here Robsjohn-Gibbings took the form of a classic klismos chair, depictions of which are found in ancient Greek paintings and sculpture, and produced a design of great elegance. Conventionalized adaptations of klismos chairs had been used in many early-nineteenth-century interiors, but this form, stripped to its essentials, goes well beyond them. It is striking in its absolute purity.

JSJ

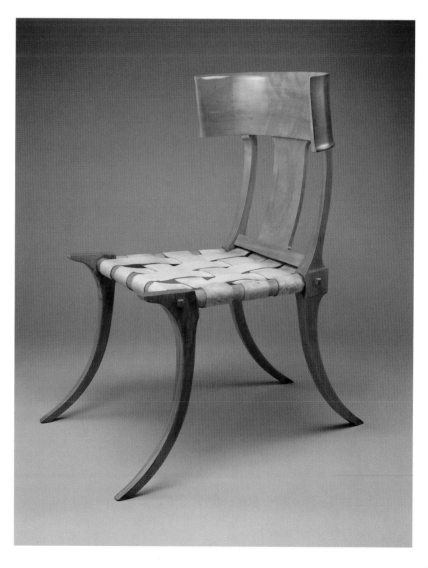

Jean Dubuffet
French, 1901–1985
Self-Portrait
1936
Oil on canvas
25 ¾ × 21 ½ in. (65.4 × 54.6 cm)
Signed and dated (upper left): J. Dubuffet / 1936
**Purchase, Gift of Mrs. Richard Rodgers,
by exchange, 2001**
2001.396

Nothing in this self-portrait identifies the thirty-five-year-old Jean Dubuffet as an artist—neither the trim haircut, the white shirt, nor the brown jacket that blends into the background. Only the intense gaze of his narrow green eyes points to the deep preoccupation of the artist, then at a crossroads in his life.

One year later Dubuffet stopped painting for the second time and returned to his wine business. Dubuffet had tried various careers. In 1918 he enrolled at the Académie Julien, in Paris, yet left after six months. Subsequently, he studied art history, languages, philosophy, literature, and music. In 1923–24 he served in the military as a meteorologist and in 1924

worked as a technical draftsman in Buenos Aires. He then became a wine merchant, first in his parents' business in Le Havre (1925–30) and then independently in Paris (1930–34 and 1937–42).

In 1942, when Dubuffet resumed painting, he repudiated his earlier style. He adopted a seemingly untutored style that defied the categories of "ugly" and "beautiful" in conventional art and that he called *art brut*.

Dubuffet gave this only surviving self-portrait to Jean Paulhan (1884–1968), a French writer, critic, and editor. In 1946 Dubuffet again celebrated their friendship in his remarkable portrait of Paulhan also in the Metropolitan (acc. no. 1999.363.20).

SR

Jacob Lawrence
American, 1917–2000
The Photographer
1942
Watercolor, gouache, and graphite on paper
22 ⅛ × 30 ½ in. (56.2 × 77.5 cm)
Signed and dated (lower right): J.LaWRENCE 42
Purchase, Lila Acheson Wallace Gift, 2001
2001.205

For nearly sixty years Jacob Lawrence was a powerful and poignant voice in American art. His historical and contemporary narratives, derived from African-American experiences, reflected the depths of humanity. Painted almost exclusively on paper with gouache and tempera, his compositions feature bold colors, matte surfaces, and naive figuration that enhance their visual and emotional impact. Urban scenes, primarily views of Harlem, were particular favorites of his and conveyed the quiet dignity of that neighborhood's citizens.

The Photographer is one of twenty pictures made in 1942 during a period of artistic and professional awakening for the twenty-five-year-old Lawrence. That year he gained national recognition when his Migration series was acquired by and divided between the Museum of Modern Art, New York, and the Phillips Collection, Washington, D.C. Also in 1942 the Metropolitan Museum purchased the first of its three works by Lawrence from its wartime "Artists for Victory" competition.

Here Lawrence suggests the sights and sounds of a busy street in Harlem filled with vehicles, pedestrians, and workers of all kinds, including an itinerant photographer under a black cloth. Mixing humor and compassion, Lawrence created a lively portrait of this vital New York community that seems to transcend specific time and place to address broader concerns about the human condition.

LMM

Robert Frank
American (b. Switzerland), b. 1924
[The Congressional]
1955
Gelatin silver print
9½ × 13 in. (24.1 × 33 cm)
Harris Brisbane Dick Fund and Dodge Fund, 2001
2001.164.4

Frank made his name by melding Walker Evans's incisive social documentation with Henri Cartier-Bresson's eye for the telling moment caught on the fly; he wielded this unified technique in the service of a particularly soulful vision that permeates his imagery with melancholy and is most eloquently inscribed in his great book, *The Americans* (1959). This photograph appeared in *Fortune* magazine, November 1955, in an article written by Evans on the Pennsylvania Railroad's clubby afternoon train, the Congressional, which ran express between New York and Washington. In a suite of images of businessmen, politicians, and lobbyists scheming, drinking, and having their shoes shined in the train's lounge, Frank focused on the rituals

and details that convey not only the social gist of the situation but, even as importantly, its undercurrent mood. These photographs provide a rare glimpse of America's power elite fed by the spoils of the country's wartime success and at ease in their mobile boardroom en route to and from the nation's capital.

JLR

63

BINGHAM COPPER MINING PIT – UTAH 73
RECLAMATION PROJECT Robert Smithson

In the two years before his sudden death, Smithson planned various land-reclamation projects to make a new form of public art from devastated industrial sites. Here he envisioned an "earthwork" that would have dwarfed even *Spiral Jetty*. In the largest open-pit copper mine in the world, Smithson proposed the construction of a huge revolving disk at the pit's base, from which to survey nature's gradual and inevitable reclamation of man's invasive enterprise—a primary theme of the picturesque tradition with which the artist was engaged. The Museum's acquisition includes not only this study but also four other important works, which together constitute the finest single representation of Smithson's work in photography.

DE

Louise Lawler
American, b. 1947
Pollock and Tureen, Arranged by Mr. and Mrs. Burton Tremaine, Connecticut
1984
Silver dye bleach print
28 × 39 in. (77.1 × 99.1 cm)
Purchase, The Horace W. Goldsmith Foundation and Jennifer and Joseph Duke Gifts, 2000
2000.434

Robert Smithson
American, 1938–1973
Bingham Copper Mining Pit—Utah Reclamation Project
1973
Photostat and plastic overlay with wax pencil
18½ × 13½ in. (47 × 34.3 cm)
Purchase, Pat and John Rosenwald Gift, 2001
2001.293

One of the most important American artists of the second half of the last century, Smithson is best known for *Spiral Jetty* (1970)—a 1,500-foot sculpture of mud, salt, and rock coiling into Utah's Great Salt Lake. Equally at home in sculpture, photography, film, and writing, Smithson simultaneously expanded our notion of art and used that expanded field to reinvigorate the great subjects, among them landscape, myth, history, and the course of civilizations.

Lawler is a spy in the house of art, casting sidelong glances at Modernist masterpieces as they wend their way from the pristine white cubes of galleries and the carpeted walls of auction houses to museum storerooms, corporate boardrooms, and private homes around the world. In its exposure of the art world's usually invisible machinery of possession, display, and circulation, Lawler's work fits comfortably within the tradition of institutional critique that began with Marcel Duchamp's *Fountain* (1917). Her effortlessly cool, deliberately neutral images are never cheap shots or tendentious sermons, however, and, as Walker Evans once wrote of Diane Arbus, there is more wonder than sociopolitical conviction in her gaze.

As sometimes happens in photography, Lawler discovered the crux of her entire project serendipitously, when she was granted access to the Connecticut home of Burton and Emily Tremaine, collectors of twentieth-century art, in 1984. Working in available light with a 35mm camera, Lawler unearthed treasures everywhere she looked, such as this decorator's duet between a late Jackson Pollock and the filigree of an eighteenth-century tureen. Simultaneously trenchant and poignant, *Pollock and Tureen* is a cutting comment laced with the love of an undercover aesthete.

DE

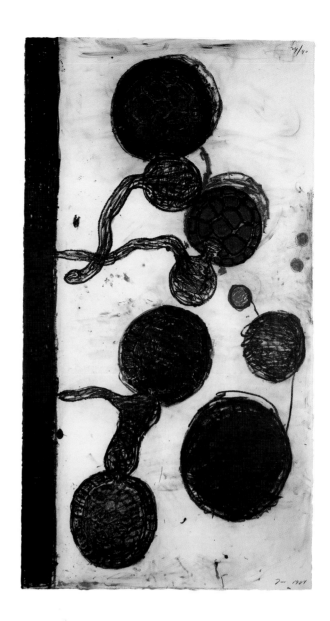

Terry Winters
American, b. 1949
Double Standard
1984
Lithograph
78 × 42 in. (198.1 × 106.7 cm)
Initialed and dated (lower right): TW 1984;
numbered (upper right): 24/40

Gift of Susan Sosnick, in memory of her husband, Robert Sosnick, 2001

2001.1.3

Best known as a painter, the New York artist Terry Winters is one of the most versatile and prolific printmakers working today. He usually bases his lithographs, intaglios, and relief prints on preliminary drawings in various media. This enormous lithograph—his largest print—shows his interest during the 1980s and early 1990s in combining abstraction with botanical, zoological, or architectural imagery. In those years Winters often hugely enlarged forms that are microscopic in nature, such as the spherical masses of fertilized ova suggested here. He has depicted the ova at the stage of embryonic growth when more and more segmentation takes place, leading to organ development. Winters rendered the cellular forms chiefly with black and nearly black lithography crayons and extended them with plantlike tendrils. This print is the earliest of thirty-seven lithographs, etchings, and woodcuts by Winters donated to the Museum this year by Susan Sosnick, whose late husband, Robert, collected the artist's work in all media. It is one of 117 prints by Winters, ranging in date from 1983 to 2001, in the Metropolitan's collection.

NR

Rachel Whiteread

British, b. 1963
Untitled (Pair)
1999
Bronze with cellulose paint
L. (a) 80¼ in. (203.8 cm); l. (b) 80½ in.
(204.5 cm)
Initialed, numbered, and dated (bottom
insides): RW 7/12 A 1999; RW 7/12 B 1999
Promised Gift of David Teiger

One of the leading British sculptors of her
generation, Whiteread is interested in themes
of memory and death. Having taken as a
starting point the sculpture *A Cast of the Space
under My Chair* (1965–68) by the American
post-Minimalist Bruce Nauman, Whiteread
first earned recognition with a full-scale con-
crete cast of the negative space—the empty
interior—of an abandoned row house in a
depressed area of East London. Her recent
public sculptures include a translucent-resin
cast of a giant water tower, installed on a
Manhattan rooftop, and the negative interior
space of a library, constructed on the Judenplatz
in Vienna as a memorial to Holocaust victims.
This work, her first in bronze, consists of
two nearly identical waist-high forms coated
with white paint. The tops of the forms, one
slightly convex, one concave, derive from
used mortuary tables purchased by Whiteread

and employed to make floor sculptures, slabs
cast in rubber. The slope of the slabs suggests
that there are drainage holes at one end of
each table. To make the antiseptic volumes
of *Untitled (Pair)* Whiteread added sides to
the slabs, creating tomblike objects that she
first installed in rows of nine pairs.

NR

Leonardo Drew

American, b. 1961
Number 24
1992
Wood, rusted and patinated iron, and cotton
waste
L. 20 ft. (6.1 m)
**Gift of Barbara Schwartz, in memory of
Eugene Schwartz, 2000**
2000.97

Working in New York City, where he studied
at Parsons and at Cooper Union, Leonardo
Drew makes large-scale metal relief sculptures that have a decidedly urban feel in their
underlying grid structure and in their use
of decaying matter from the city's streets.
While the actual constructions are completely
abstract in design, the artist's unorthodox
materials (rusted metal, cotton waste, rope,
cardboard boxes, and discarded debris) have
inherent narrative associations that often
relate to his African-American identity. In
Number 24, for example, the row of rusted
brown metal beams, jagged and dangerous,
suggests the condition of run-down ghetto
neighborhoods and tenement buildings,
while the white tufts of cotton, scattered
across the surface like drifting snow, allude
to slavery and the plantations of the South.
Such references, however, are left vague so
that viewers may relate them to their own set
of experiences. Finding meaning and even
beauty in apparent flaws and ugliness, the
sculptor welcomes the visual contradictions
posed by his materials (hard versus soft, dark
versus light, solid versus ephemeral). Since
his first solo gallery exhibition in New York
in 1992 (which included *Number 24*), Drew's
work has received national attention.

LMM

Rineke Dijkstra
Dutch, b. 1959
Kolbrzeg, Poland
1992
Chromogenic print
47 ⅝ × 39 ¾ in. (121 × 101 cm)
Purchase, Roy R. and Marie S. Neuberger Foundation Inc., Jennifer and Joseph Duke, Gary and Sarah Wolkowitz and Anne Marie MacDonald Gifts, 2001
2001.307

Between 1992 and 1996 Dijkstra produced a celebrated series of full-length portraits of teenagers on various beaches in Poland, Croatia, Ukraine, Belgium, England, and the United States, describing the liminal state of adolescence with startling eloquence. Posing her young subjects before a luminous background of sand, sea, and sky, she imbued the portraits with an elemental, almost mythic quality that seems to transcend the carefully observed particulars of national identity and class.

In this photograph a skinny Polish girl in a lime green bathing suit confronts the camera with a heartbreaking blend of awkwardness and studied nonchalance. Standing at the ocean's edge, she tilts her head and slips unconsciously into a classical contrapposto pose. Dijkstra captures this moment with her camera, deftly revealing the eternal within the everyday. Shot from a low angle against a darkening sky, the girl appears simultaneously large and small—monumental yet vulnerable, half exposed, half grown, halfway between innocence and experience. With its perfectly modulated blend of clarity and ambiguity, the photograph is a stunning depiction of Venus at the awkward age.

MF

George Segal
American, 1924–2000
Self-Portrait
1998
Charcoal and pastel on paper
50 ⅛ × 38 ¼ in. (127.3 × 97.2 cm)
Signed and dated (lower left): G Segal 7-98
Purchase, Mr. and Mrs. Samuel H. Lindenbaum Gift, 2001
2001.57

George Segal, one of America's most important postwar sculptors, is best known for the anonymous white cast-plaster figures he often placed in real environments. Gaining recognition in the Pop Art era of the 1960s, he frequently tied his subjects to popular culture and contemporary events. This exceptional late drawing, however, reveals another, more personal side of the artist's talents and is part of a series of larger-than-life, black-and-white heads of family and friends that he began in the 1990s. Executed with hundreds of strokes of black charcoal and pastel, this last self-portrait (at age seventy-five) is a tour de force of expressionist drawing that presents a powerful, intimate view of his psychological state and aging physiognomy. Looming out of the darkness to a height of almost four feet, Segal's craggy features fill nearly the entire composition, yet they project an innate humanness that contradicts their monumental scale. The dramatic chiaroscuro effect he achieved with bright lighting and deep shadows gives the likeness a strong sculptural quality. Gazing intently into the viewer's space, the artist seems to be assessing some unseen presence—perhaps his own reflection. LMM

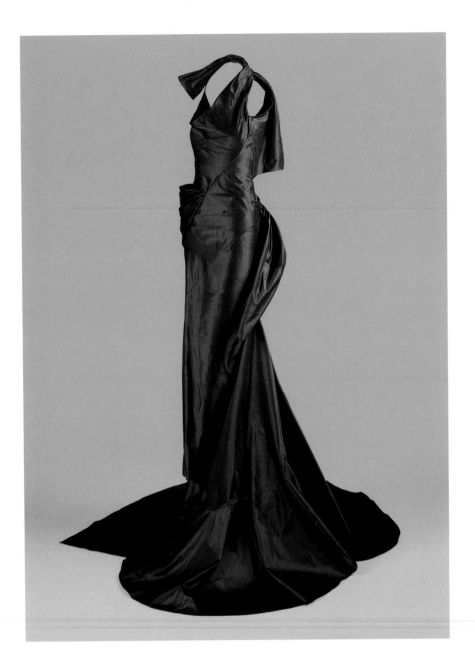

John Galliano (designer)
British, b. 1960
Christian Dior (couturier)
French (Paris), est. 1947
Evening Gown
Spring/Summer 2000
Silk taffeta
L. (center back) 57 in. (144.8 cm)
Gift of Anne E. de la Renta, 2001
2001.397

In this gown from John Galliano's controversial "Hobo" collection for Dior, extravagant, changeable silk taffeta is whipped into a spiraling vortex. The naturally stiff "hand" of taffeta and the virtuosity of the Dior atelier contribute to this illusion of fabric come to life. From neckline to train, four parallel panels, each longer than the next, are angled into a body-conforming bias. The gown recalls both the aerodynamic sleekness of the 1930s, in its second-skin fit, and the 1950s illustrations by René Gruau of fabric snaking around bodies and spinning into space.

Here, as in many of Galliano's creations, the merging of diverse sources has resulted in a design less grafted together than crosspollinated into a new hybrid. Over the years, whether the references have been to *les merveilleuses* of the Directoire, courtesans of the Belle Époque, or sophisticates of between-the-wars café society, Galliano has consistently assimilated the styles and sensibilities of the past into convincing contemporary glamour. While his creations are generally apolitical and ahistorical—the result of an intuitive, primarily visual synthesis—an implicit social critique may be read in this confection of haute couture, inspired by the rag-swaddled image of a Parisian tramp.

HK

Geoffrey Beene
American, b. 1927
Evening Gown
Fall/Winter 1993
Leather and wool jersey
L. (center back) 60 in. (152.4 cm)
Gift of Geoffrey Beene, 2001
2001.393.118

The recent work of Geoffrey Beene has been characterized by an increasingly sensual reductivism. In this evening gown an asymmetrical yoke in black leather acknowledges the anatomy—the clavicle, sternum, and spine—while also evoking another reference, that of a shoulder holster, in its trapezoidal shape, strapping, and use of material. As in many of Beene's designs, the yoke is a detail simultaneously abstract and allusive, a vestige of earlier collections in which harnesses appeared as separate accessories to overlay, segment, and define the torso.

A subtle provocative intent has always percolated through the designer's collections. Here Beene refutes precedent and resists convention when he employs gray wool jersey and black leather, materials generally consigned to day- or sportswear. Cut in one piece, with only a center-back seam, the body of the gown reveals Beene's essentially Minimalist strategy. Still, like an architectural detail by Santiago Calatrava, whose work is characterized by zoomorphic bone- and riblike vaults, Beene's supporting yoke introduces a decorative flourish through its arcing organicism. The American designer reveals, as does the Spanish architect in his elegant engineering of shapes, an advocacy of Modernism's expressive functionalism.

HK

Magdalena Abakanowicz
Polish, b. 1930
Figure on a Trunk
2000
Bronze
W. 8 ft. 7 in. (2.6 m)
Joseph H. Hazen Foundation Purchase Fund, 2000
2000.348a, b

Throughout four decades the human condition has been a constant concern for the Polish artist Magdalena Abakanowicz, who lives and works in Warsaw. This over-lifesize, headless figure cast in bronze embodies, in a single form, the unique expressiveness and powerful presence of all of her sculpture. Standing firmly at the midpoint of a beam, which balances upon two log-shaped cylinders, this convex shell of a figure, of no specific sex, looms large. Abakanowicz's sculptures of humans are often positioned in groups—ranging from a dozen to more than 150—and are typically headless, conveying the loss of individuality, an increasing occurrence in modern society. Here the elevated solitary figure, though headless, seems to look to a far horizon above the viewer's plane.

In 1999 an earlier cast of this sculpture was included in the "Abakanowicz on the Roof" installation on the Museum's Iris and B. Gerald Cantor Roof Garden. After the close of that exhibition, the artist offered to produce an additional cast for the Metropolitan's collection. The sculpture's surface was finished by the artist's own hand, contributing to its uniqueness. *Androgyne III,* a similar but seated headless figure by Abakanowicz, was acquired by the Museum in 1986 (acc. no. 1986.221a, b).

ALS

Stephen Hannock
American, b. 1951
**The Oxbow: After Church, after Cole,
Flooded (Flooded River for the
Matriarchs E. & A. Mongan), Green
Light**
2000
Acrylic with oil glazes on canvas
96 × 144 in. (243.8 × 365.8 cm)
**Purchase, Moore Capital Management Inc.
Gift, 2001**
2001.153

Stephen Hannock captured this view of the
Connecticut River from the same vantage
point chosen by Thomas Cole (1801–1848)
for his famous *View from Mount Holyoke,
Northampton, Massachusetts, after a Thunder-
storm—The Oxbow* (1836), in the collection
of the American Wing of the Metropolitan
Museum (acc. no. 08.228).

The lacquered surface and transparent
light effects of Hannock's painting emphasize
the stillness of dusk on a cloudless autumn
day. No breath of wind stirs the air; no

animal enlivens this panoramic landscape
combining truth with fantasy. In the 1920s
a passage was cut through the river's once-
scenic loop, the Oxbow, and bridges now
connect the mainland and the artificially created island. The mountains rising in the blue
distance are invented, as is the flooded state
of the river.

Since attending art classes at Smith College,
in Northampton, during the 1970s, Hannock
has claimed this landscape as his own. Here it
inspired him to cover large areas of the rust-
colored, tilled fields with inscriptions that
relate to his friends and to the events of daily
life. The names and initials in the title refer
to Cole's student Frederic E. Church (1826–
1900) and to Agnes Mongan (1905–1998) and
her sister Elizabeth (b. 1905), both important
curators and teachers, as well as mentors of
the artist.   SR

Brice Marden
American, b. 1938
Red Line Muses
2001
Etching and lithograph
22 × 30 in. (55.9 × 76.2 cm)
John B. Turner Fund, 2001
2001.117

Since his student days at Yale University in
the 1960s, Marden has been engaged in print-
making, creating finely rendered etchings and
silkscreens akin to Minimalism in their cool
touch. However, his aesthetic is not easily
categorized; it transcends succinct labels in its
embrace of the spiritual as well as in its varied
formal influences. By the mid-1980s Marden
had turned away from his signature planes of
pure color and tightly knit geometric lines in
favor of an open, fluid use of line inspired by
forms of Eastern calligraphy.

One of seven prints recently executed in
etching and lithograph at Gemini G.E.L.,
in Los Angeles, *Red Line Muses* evolves from
Marden's interest in calligraphic gesture.

His broad, ribbonlike strokes extend languorously to the edges of the plate and are overlaid with a layer of hastily scratched lines, which are printed in muted celadon and neatly framed by a fine red border. The translucent layers of contrasting marks produce a subtle sense of pictorial depth without spoiling the rich surface effect of the print.

SJR

Joel Shapiro
American, b. 1941
Untitled
2000–2001
Cast aluminum with oil paint
H. 12 ft. (3.7 m)
Signed and stamped (in cast-aluminum plate welded to inside wall of lowest element): Joel Shapiro 1/4 2001
Partial and Promised Gift of Dee Dee and Herb Glimcher, 2001
2001.201

Joel Shapiro's sculptures of the 1970s in cast iron, limestone, or wood were in part responses to earlier Minimalist "specific objects" by artists such as Donald Judd and Carl André. Shapiro absorbed their geometric vocabulary of assembled parts, itself in the tradition of Russian Constructivist sculpture, yet he rejected their neutrality and pure abstraction. Shapiro wished his works to be read metaphorically, as allusions that could draw on the viewer's memories and reactions to imagery suggesting figures. This buoyant

dancing object, nearly twice lifesize, is the first sculpture by Shapiro to enter the Museum's collection and his first cast sculpture painted red. It consists of five hexahedral elements. The two "arms" and two "legs" are square in section, and the fifth, torsolike element between them is rectangular. The hollow aluminum lengths were bolted together at acute or obtuse angles and reinforced internally with stainless steel. The aluminum elements were sand cast from solid lengths of wood that Shapiro joined, following smaller wooden models. He left the channels made by the saw, rather than smoothing them out, as evidence of his cutting and casting process.

NR

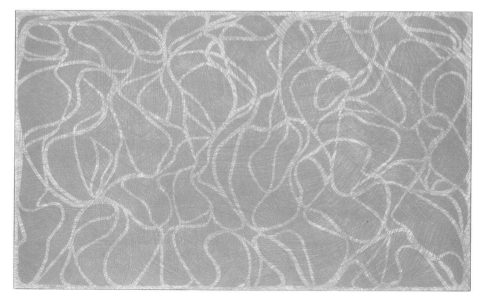

71

Headdress Ornament

Peru (Sihuas), 100 B.C.–A.D. 300(?)
Gold
H. 11¼ in. (28.6 cm)
**Purchase, Discovery Communications Inc.
Gift, 2001**
2001.32

Precious-metal objects from the south coast
of Peru are rare compared to those found on
the north coast, where deposits were more
abundant and accessible in ancient times.
Usually of modest proportions and invariably
made of hammered sheet gold, south-coast
works are distinctive in form and surface decoration. This object is part of a group of ornaments that are exceptional for their large size
and have the same shape and similar overall
repoussé designs. They are usually attributed
to the Nazca culture; however, recent research
suggests that they may come from the Camaná
and Sihuas valleys, on the far south coast,
where independent traditions flourished. The
iconography focuses on a stylized, oblong
frontal face repeated at different scales, with
circular eyes and what appear to be mus-
taches and short beards. Rows of circles of
various dimensions and zigzag lines fill the
spaces between the faces. Two pairs of perfo-
rations on either side of the central face suggest that the object may have been worn
affixed to a turban or a headdress, although
there are no depictions in the art of the region
to confirm this use. Perhaps such works were
not intended to be worn in life, but rather
were attached to burial shrouds or mummy
bundles, which were then placed in tombs.

HK

William Ellis
British, 1794–1872
Antsahatsiroa (Madagascar)
1862–65
Albumen print from collodion negative
7½ × 6½ in. (19.1 × 16.5 cm)
**Purchase, The Fred and Rita Richman
Foundation Gift and Rogers Fund, 2000**
2000.608

Reverend William Ellis, a prominent member
of the London Missionary Society, made this
exquisite view of Antsahatsiroa, Madagascar.
He established his reputation in Hawaii and
Tahiti during the early 1820s and was the first
European in those places to translate, print,
and illustrate Christian scriptures in local languages. In London, in 1853, Ellis heard that
the rulers of Madagascar were again amicable
to missionaries, and he prepared to travel
there for the society (he eventually visited
three times). Ellis was fully aware of the
power of the printed word and image, and
that year, at the age of fifty-nine, he embraced
photography. He received technical advice in
London from the prominent photographer
Roger Fenton. In Madagascar Ellis joined his
society colleague James Cameron, a photographer who had been among the first group
of British missionaries to travel to the island
in 1826 and was now fluent in the Malagasy
language. Ellis's first attempts in 1853–54 to visit

the rulers at Antananarivo with a camera were not successful, but he returned to the capital in 1856 to make portraits of some of Madagascar's royalty. Ellis was not the first missionary to take photographs in the capital but was possibly second to a Jesuit, Father Finaz. However, those daguerreotypes have never been located; thus Ellis's photographs of Madagascar are some of the earliest in existence.

VLW

Mask
Indonesia (Timor Island, possibly East Timor), 19th–early 20th century
Wood, fiber, and paint, with traces of lime
H. 9⅛ in. (23 cm)
Purchase, Discovery Communications Inc. Gift and Rogers Fund, 2000
2000.444

Timorese dance masks are one of several distinctive masking traditions practiced by the peoples of eastern Indonesia. Found primarily in East Timor, they represent distant ancestors and were worn by warriors during victory celebrations and probably at other important feasts and ceremonies. The masks were often painted and adorned with bristles or strips of hide representing facial hair. The holes in the upper lip and forehead of this example likely served for the attachment of a mustache and eyebrows, while the wearer would have looked out through the mouth. When in use, the mask would have been attached to a hood of fur or cloth that

covered the remainder of the head and concealed the dancer's identity. While some masks made of more perishable materials would have been discarded at the conclusion of the ceremony, wooden ones, such as this highly polished and deeply patinated work, were preserved and reused for many years.

EK

Ancestor Effigy (Rambaramp)
Vanuatu (Malakula, Tomman Island), mid-20th century
Fiber, bamboo, wood, bone, and paint
H. 6 ft. 9 in. (2.1 m)
Gift of Ms. Terry Beck, 2000
2000.615

The imposing ancestor effigies, or *rambaramp,* of southern Malakula, in Vanuatu, are among the most visually striking of the island's diverse sculptural traditions. Each depicts a prominent recently deceased individual whose spirit has joined the ranks of the ancestors, the powers of which ensure the well-being of the

community. The spirit itself resides in the skull, which forms the head of the image and is covered with a papier-mâché-like paste of finely chopped plant fiber to create a portrait of the individual in life. The body consists of the same material laid over a framework of bamboo, wood, and fibrous leaves.

Southern Malakulan societies practiced a complex system of progressive religious initiations, and only individuals who achieved the highest levels, or "grades," were entitled to have their spirits reside in a *rambaramp*. This example from Tomman Island, off the southern coast of Malakula, commemorates a man who had undergone nine of a possible eleven grade initiations during his lifetime. The "herringbone" body designs, elaborate shoulder projections, and shell trumpets clutched in the hands mark his exalted status. The mask-like faces represent idealized supernatural beings and combine features of humans with those of the sacred pigs revered throughout Vanuatu.

EK

Couple
Madagascar (Menabe region, Sakalava peoples),
17th–late 18th century
Wood
H. 39 in. (99 cm)
**Purchase, Lila Acheson Wallace, Daniel
and Marian Malcolm, and James J. Ross
Gifts, 2001**
2001.408

This Madagascar couple ranks as the fore-
most artistic achievement of a region at the
confluence of African and Pacific Island aesthetic influences. Its quiet power and lyrically
balanced symmetry have made it one of the
rare works from southeastern Africa to have
had an impact on Western art. Created as the
finial of a freestanding exterior monument,
this sculpture appears to have been designed as
a pair with one in the Louvre that is attributed
to the same artist. The Metropolitan's work
was known in Paris by the early twentieth century and entered the collection of the British
sculptor Sir Jacob Epstein about 1922–23.

The idea of the fundamental complemen-
tarity of man and woman that is so eloquently
depicted in this iconic image is an important
theme in Malagasy spiritual life. In this representation the man is only slightly taller than
his female companion, who balances a vessel
on her head. Although frozen in a posture in
which their calves are fused with the base of
the capital while their hands are held to their
sides, they appear poised to come to life. The
immediacy of the representation is under-
scored by their intense facial expressions,
which are dominated by deeply recessed eye
sockets that engage the viewer.

AL

Male Corset
Sudan (Dinka peoples), 2nd half of 20th century
Glass, fur, shell, and vegetable fiber
L. (a) (center back) 30 in. (76.2 cm);
l. (b) (center back) 16 in. (40.6 cm)
Isabel Shults Fund, 2001
2001.177a, b

This extraordinary beaded corset is a rare example of the everyday wear of Dinka men. Because the Dinka peoples are herders, wandering the vast plains of southern Sudan, portable possessions are very important. Like many southern and eastern African cultures, the Dinka have traditionally focused on the human form as the primary method of artistic expression.

Because these garments are used to communicate characteristics such as gender, age, wealth, and ethnic affiliation, we can infer a significant amount of information about the past wearer of this object. In particular, the red-and-black patterning indicates that the corset was worn by a male between the ages of fifteen and twenty-five. The decoration of cowries, along with the extreme height of the back, marks the wearer as someone of considerable wealth. The addition of the fur skirt (possibly cattle hair) is significant. The Dinka, who have traditionally gained their livelihood from their herds, value their animals as a source of aesthetic inspiration and a link to the spiritual world.

As highly prized commodities, beads are a sign of wealth and status among the Dinka peoples. The polychrome glass beads that make up this garment are European, while the cowries and fur skirt are undoubtedly of local origin. EM

Guanyin's lean physique and full, but not fleshy, face suggest a date in the early part of the twelfth century. The bodhisattva wears a long skirt and full shawl, a thin scarf knotted at his chest, an elaborate pectoral, and an armlet. A thin fillet, which supported a diadem, encircles his parted and braided hair. The hair, the textile-like designs on the edges of the shawl, and the lion's mane, fur, and tail are all treated schematically, in accordance with the rhythm of the overall composition.

This elegant sculpture is one of two early Chinese representations of Guanyin of the Lion's Roar. The other, made of iron and dated 1112, is in the collection of the Kyoto National Museum, Japan.

DPL

Zhang Jizhi
Chinese, 1186–1266
Excerpt from "Song of Leyou Park"
Southern Song dynasty (1127–1279)
Section of handscroll mounted as hanging scroll; ink on paper
12¾ × 30⅛ in. (32.4 × 76.5 cm)
Gift of Sylvan Barnet and William Burto, 2000
2000.325

Zhang Jizhi, the last important Song calligrapher, was admired for his large-character writing, with its boldly contrasting blunt and sinuous brushstrokes and fluid ligatures that trace the movement of the brush tip between strokes. This work is the only example of Zhang's large-scale calligraphy outside of Asia.

Although Zhang attained the top civil-service rank, he never held a high office. His fame as a calligrapher, however, spread to the Jin empire in northern China and to Japan, where his writing was prized by Zen monks. This piece was once part of a long handscroll, transcribing a poem by Du Fu (712–770), that was carried to Japan and cut into sections for display in a tokonoma. An outstanding example of Zhang's large regular script, it was venerated primarily for its aesthetic qualities. This section was cut in such a manner that the phrasing of the original was lost. The two couplets from which the segment comes may be translated as follows (the text of the scroll is in italics):

Bodhisattva Seated on a Lion
Chinese, Song (960–1127) or Jin (1115–1234) dynasty, 11th–early 13th century
Poplar with traces of polychrome pigments
H. 42⅛ in. (107 cm)
Purchase, The Dillon Fund Gift, in honor of Brooke Astor, 2000
2000.270

The upraised right and lowered left legs, as well as the lionlike mount, identify the sculpture as Guanyin (in Sanskrit, Avalokiteshvara), the Bodhisattva of Compassion. After the tenth century this posture, known as "royal ease," was standard in representations of Guanyin in his paradise, believed to be Mount Putuo, an island off the coast of southeast China. The mount indicates that the sculpture represents Guanyin of the Lion's Roar (Simhanada Avalokiteshvara). The roar symbolizes both a moment of transcendent understanding and the bodhisattva's supernal wisdom. Later Chinese images of Guanyin riding a creature identified as a *hou,* meaning "roar," may derive from this traditional manifestation.

Palace gates, open beneath clear skies,
  reveal a vast expanse;
By the Serpentine *are kingfisher curtains
  arrayed with silver plaques.*
Skimming the water, back and forth, the
  dancers' sleeves flutter;
Climbing to the clouds, crisp and clear,
  the singers' voices rise.

MKH

Wang Hui
Chinese, 1632–1717
Yang Jin
Chinese, 1644–1728
Gu Fang
Chinese, active ca. 1690–1720
Wang Yun
Chinese, 1652–after 1735
Xu Mei
Chinese, active ca. 1690–1722
Landscapes after Ancient Masters
*Qing dynasty (1644–1911), Kangxi period
(1662–1722), dated 1692*
*Album of sixteen paintings; ink and color on
paper*
Each 11 × 12⅛ in. (27.9 × 30.8 cm)
**Gift of Marie-Hélène and Guy A. Weill,
2000**
2000.665.2

In 1691 Wang Hui, the leading artist of his
day, was summoned to Beijing to oversee the
creation of a mammoth imperial commission
documenting the Kangxi emperor's southern
inspection tour of 1689. The painting, con-
sisting of twelve monumental handscrolls, is
the largest pictorial work of the Qing dynasty.
(The Metropolitan owns one scroll from this
set; acc. no. 1979.5.) Since the finished set
bears no artists' signatures or seals, it is only
through group works such as the Museum's
new acquisition that the identity of Wang's
artistic team can be established. The album,
in which four younger artists from Wang's
home region practiced the methods of ancient
artists, is a rare example of a master painter's

having recruited assistants and shaped their
style to conform to the orthodox manner,
which epitomized scholarly taste at that time.
This academic style became the hallmark of
all later Qing court commissions.

The leaf illustrated here, *Mountain Water-
fall,* is by Wang Hui's leading disciple, Yang
Jin, who has inscribed it with a poem:

For ten days spring clouds have obscured
  the stream's source;
In the middle of the night a west wind
  brings rain to the [mountain's] foot.
But I feel the urgent thunder roar in the
  empty valley,
So from a distance I know that the myriad
  gorges are competing in their flows.

MKH

Twelve-Panel Screen

*Chinese, Qing dynasty (1644–1911), Kangxi
period (1662–1722), late 17th century
Mother-of-pearl, lacquer, and gold-foil inlay
(recto); colored lacquer and paint (verso)
9 ft. 4½ in. × 24 ft. 8 in. (2.9 × 7.5 m)*
**Purchase, The Vincent Astor Foundation
Gift, 2001**
2001.76a–l

The use of mother-of-pearl for inlaid decoration on lacquer is common to the eastern seaboard of the Asian continent and to Japan. In China this type of decoration is known from about the eighth century B.C. In the early twelfth century A.D. extremely thin shells of the haliotis (abalone), which have a high degree of iridescence, began to be used. Lacquer inlaid with mother-of-pearl reached its peak of refinement in the seventeenth century, and this recently acquired large screen provides an excellent example. The domestic scenes in a palatial setting are depicted in mosaics of minute pieces of shell, oriented in various directions to produce a polychrome effect. Gold foil is used for highlights. The walls and rocks are rendered in crushed shells, creating a shimmering appearance.

The verso is decorated in colored lacquer and oil-based pigments with a multitude of birds among blossoming trees and flowers. The pictorial style and subject matter of the decoration on both sides are closely related to those of contemporaneous woodblock prints.

JCYW

Recto (detail)

Recto (detail)

Verso (detail)

that encircle her wrists. Above, another triad of sacred jewels rests on an open lotus, flanked by Chinese symbols of the complementary forces of sun and moon.

This transformation of the wrathful Hindu deva Dakini emerged within Esoteric Buddhism in Japan. Originally a man-eating demoness, she was converted by the Vairocana Buddha into a powerful life-engendering deity. In the complex interaction of Buddhism, Shinto, and Taoist yin-yang practices in medieval Japan, this icon embodied near-magical powers of fecundity that were invoked not only in enthronement rituals but also in personal contexts. The mantra identified with this deity was chanted to achieve control over the mind. Medieval tales recount invocations of Dakiniten by both men and women to win position and favor at court, as well as in matters of the heart.

BBF

Plate

Chinese, Qing dynasty (1644–1911), ca. 1st third of 18th century
"Chinese Imari"–style ware; porcelain painted in underglaze blue and overglaze polychrome enamels
Diam. 19½ in. (49.5 cm)
Gift of Michael L. Rosenberg, 2001
2001.362

This plate is a splendid example of the fusion of Chinese and Japanese tastes that is sometimes found in Chinese ceramics produced during the early years of the eighteenth century. A distinctive five-claw imperial dragon chasing a flaming pearl, which exemplifies early-eighteenth-century Chinese dragons at their finest, commands the center of this impressive porcelain. The creature is improbably juxtaposed with an unmistakably Japanese-style border design, in which undulating lines form cloud-shaped cartouches containing bold *kiku* chrysanthemum sprays.

The preeminent Jingdezhen kiln complexes in China's Jiangxi Province had been challenged by the commercial success of the so-called Imari porcelains that were being exported in quantity to Europe from kilns in Arita, Japan. Accordingly, they appropriated the Imari palette of underglaze blue, overglaze iron red, and gold, as well as many of

the Imari designs, for the decoration of their own "Chinese Imari" porcelains.

In a further step enamels from the Chinese *famille verte* palette were occasionally added to the primary colors of Imari porcelains to create a new category of "Chinese Imari"–style wares. In still another variant of this type of decoration, seen here, the gold of the original Japanese palette could be completely omitted.

SGV

Dakiniten

Japanese, Nambokuchō period (1333–92)
Hanging scroll; ink, color, and gold on hemp
29½ × 13 in. (74.9 × 33 cm)
Purchase, Friends of Asian Art Gifts, in honor of Wen C. Fong, 2000
2000.274

As though a sudden apparition, a female deity in fluttering raiment splashes up a frame of foam on a billowing sea. Riding a white fox on a cloud held aloft by a pair of dragons, she clenches a *vajra* (thunderbolt) surmounted by a sword, a symbol of Buddhist power. In her palm she cradles a triad of sacred jewels, and others are scattered around her as abundant blessings. In her crown are auspicious protectors of the harvest: diminutive foxes on coiled white snakes, like those

Mandala of Han'nya Bosatsu

*Japanese, Muromachi period (1392–1573),
16th century
Hanging scroll; ink, color, and gold on silk
Image 64½ × 48⅝ in. (163.9 × 123.5 cm)*

**Gift of Mary and Jackson Burke
Foundation, 2000**

2000.289

This large hanging scroll depicts one of the
most important Buddhist deities, Han'nya
Bosatsu (in Sanskrit, Prajnaparamita Bodhisattva), the embodiment of transcendental
knowledge and perfect wisdom. Han'nya
Bosatsu is only rarely represented at the center of a mandala. The triad of the *bosatsu,*
seated on a lotus pedestal on the back of a
lion, flanked by two standing figures, Bonten
(Brahma) and Taishakuten (Indra)—originally Hindu gods—inhabits the innermost
precinct. The *bosatsu*'s sixteen protectors
(*jūroku zenshin*) are more loosely distributed
within the surrounding register. Far from
the center of divinity in the outer register,
carefree demonic guardians (*kijin*) guard each
of the sixteen protectors. Directional gates at
the centers of the sides provide entry from
the secular to the sacred. Heavenly music-
making beings (*hiten*) around the canopy
celebrate Han'nya Bosatsu. At the bottom,
in the center of the outermost register, is the
figure of a monk at worship, evoking the
physical world of time and space. Dragons
and a phoenix along the outermost borders
serve to protect the entire abstract realm.
Mandalas like this one were necessary
accoutrements for rituals dedicated to the
attainment of greater wisdom.

MW

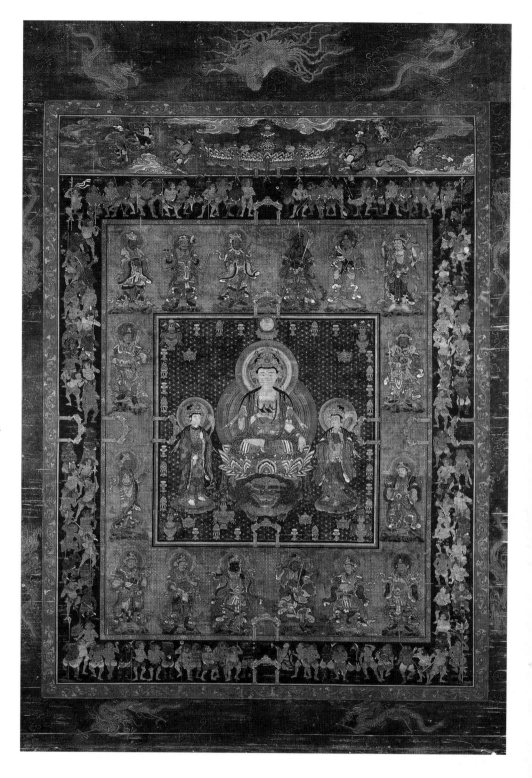

Detail

impart a sense of auspicious connection to a great tradition. Although in practice the dances are performed singly in slow, dramatic movements set to stately music, their random placement and simultaneous appearance within the solid gold field on this screen convey a sense of joyous plenty in keeping with the propitious nature of the theme. At left musicians play drums, flutes, and a mouth organ on a dais covered by a large brocade awning. The poses and costumes are based on pictorial scrolls that transmitted the classic repertory.

The artist Yasunobu established an important branch of the Kano school in Edo (Tokyo). His large signature at upper left includes a title, Hōgen Eishin (Honorable Eishin), which he was awarded in 1662 and used until his death in 1685.

BBF

Saddle (Kura)
Japanese, Edo period (1615–1868), dated 1658
Wood, lacquer, abalone shell, and gold
L. 14½ in. (36.8 cm)
Purchase, Morihiro and Sumiko Ogawa Gift, in memory of Dr. Sato Kanzan, 2000
2000.405

Japanese saddles are distinguished by an ingeniously simple method of construction combined with a virtually inexhaustible range of decorative motifs. The construction consists, typically, of only four pieces of skillfully

Kano Yasunobu
Japanese, 1613–1685
Bugaku Dancers
Edo period (1615–1868), 1662–65
One of a pair of 6-panel folding screens; mineral colors, ink, and gold on gold-leafed paper
5 ft. 9⅜ in. × 12 ft. 2⅜ in. (1.8 × 3.7 m)
Gift of James L. Greenfield, in memory of Margaret Greenfield, 2000
2000.453

Exotic costumes, masks, and stylized movement mark the ritual dances known as bugaku, which have been customary at court and shrine festivals in Japan since the eighth century. Many of the dances preserve Chinese Tang-dynasty (618–907) forms adopted in the eighth century by the Nara court, but others have roots in Japan, Korea, and Southeast Asia. Performed on important occasions to please and pacify the gods, they

shaped wood, which are held together by mortise-and-tenon joints and fastened in place by hemp or leather lacing. The surfaces are covered in Japanese lacquer (*urushi*) and often incorporate designs in gold or silver and inlays of ivory, mother-of-pearl, or abalone shell. This saddle is a particularly fine example of black-and-gold lacquer with extensive abalone-shell inlay. It is especially distinctive, as it is possibly the only example with inlay of this kind that is signed, dated, and made for a known family. The underside is marked with the as-yet-unidentified *kao* (seal or monogram) of the saddle maker and with the date *Meireki yon sai* (equivalent to 1658). The outside of the pommel and cantle is decorated in gold with the *mon* (heraldic insignia) of the Nishio family, daimyo of Yokosuka, in present-day Shizuoka Prefecture. Delicate inlay covers much of the saddle and features designs of billowing waves (*seikaiha*) and round blossoms set among lush scrolling vines (*karakusa*).

DJL

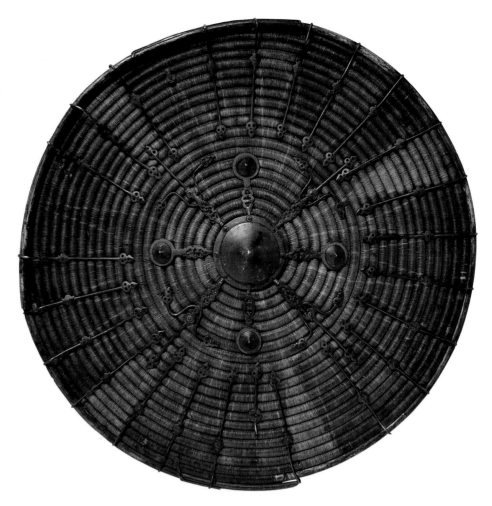

Cane Shield with Iron Fittings

Tibetan, 14th–16th century
Wood, iron, and brass
Diam. 29⅞ in. (75.9 cm)
Purchase, Arthur Ochs Sulzberger Gift, 2001
2001.55

Cane shields are made of tight concentric rings of narrow, spirally wound wooden rods. They were widely used in both Persia and Turkey up to the eighteenth century and are well represented in Islamic art and by many surviving examples. It is less well known, however, that distinctive types of cane shields were also employed, perhaps from as early as the fourteenth century, in Tibet, where they remained as military equipment until the early twentieth century and for ceremonial purposes as late as the 1950s. Despite their longevity, Tibetan cane shields with pierced and decorated iron fittings are extremely rare. The quality and complexity of their iron fittings vary widely. The fittings are both ornamental and practical: They strengthen the shield by making it more rigid. This example is one of the best preserved and more elaborate of its type. The iron fittings are closely related to those found on Tibetan leather boxes, certain types of wooden furniture, and a few rare examples of leather armor. The shield is

important, therefore, not only in terms of the history of Tibetan arms and armor, but also for its relationship to Tibetan metalwork and other decorative arts.

DJL

Twenty-Five Initiation Cards (Tsakalis)

Tibetan, late 13th to mid-14th century
Opaque watercolor on paper
Each 6¼ × 5¾ in. (15.9 × 14.6 cm)
Rogers Fund, 2000
2000.282.1–.25

This small painting is part of a set that was probably used during Buddhist initiation ceremonies. Each has a letter on the back that indicates the sequence in which the set is organized. The first group forms a meditation mandala. It is centered on the five Tathāgatas, or celestial Buddhas, and has four "gate-keepers" (guardians of the directions) stationed at its perimeter. In this group all of the deities of the mandala are associated with Vajrasattva, the sixth and ultimate Buddha. The bodhisattva Samantabhadra and his

consort, Samantabhadri, who appear on individual cards, indicate that the set was probably made for the Nyingma (Elder) school of Tibetan Buddhism. The next two cards were employed during the actual initiation rite, while the last group corresponds to the six realms of being. Uncharacteristically for *tsakalis,* the cards are painted in the Nepalese style, probably by a Newar artist.

SMK

2000.282.16

A Selection from the Samuel Eilenberg Collection

Southeast Asian (Thailand and Indonesia), Bronze and Iron Ages, ca. 500 B.C.–A.D. 300
Bronze and earthenware
H. (large container) 8⅞ in. (22.5 cm)

Samuel Eilenberg Collection, Bequest of Samuel Eilenberg, 1998

2000.284.55, .42, .41; .53a, b; .47

In Samuel Eilenberg's major gift of sixty-seven South and Southeast Asian works of art, including Chola-period (846–1279) sculptures and other Indian and Pakistani works, the most significant part, in terms of art history and the needs of our collection, dates from the Southeast Asian Bronze and Iron Ages (ca. 500 B.C.–A.D. 300). Older than the earliest Buddhist and Hindu bronze sculptures from Southeast Asia, the objects in the Eilenberg Collection demonstrate the superb craftsmanship and technological expertise developed early on in the area.

This Bronze Age culture is usually referred to as the "Dongson," after a village in northern Vietnam excavated by French archaeologists in the 1930s. Parallel Bronze Age cultures in Indonesia and Thailand share a vocabulary of similar motifs and shapes, which range

from large bronze drums, often with figural decorations, found mostly in Vietnam, to the more widely distributed bracelets and other objects with bold spiral designs. There is also a stylistic affiliation with bronzes of the Dian kingdom in Yunnan, China.

The Eilenberg gift, along with a few important "Dongson"-culture bronzes acquired from other sources, makes the Museum's collection virtually unrivaled in the Western world for the study of this material.

ML

Standing Female Deity

Cambodian, Pre-Angkor period, style of Prasat Andet, ca. last quarter of 7th–beginning of 8th century
Stone
H. 52¾ in. (134 cm)
Purchase, Rogers Fund and Anonymous Gift, in honor of Martin Lerner, 2000
2000.531

This wonderful female deity, probably the Hindu goddess Durga, not only broadens exponentially the range of the Museum's Cambodian collection but adds a new dimension to our Southeast Asian holdings. It is the largest and most important Pre-Angkor-period (6th–early 9th century) sculpture of a female deity to appear on the market in more than thirty years.

The four-armed deity wears a cylindrical miter and a long sarong. This garment is secured at the waist, and the cloth hanging down in front doubles over and is tucked in at the waist, forming a looped drapery motif.

The conception of the female form—slim-waisted and full-bodied, with ample breasts and thighs suggestive of fecundity and potential motherhood—follows early Indian precedents. Here the large, full, taut breasts and the youthful face indicate a female just reaching maturity. The posture is subtle, with a projecting right knee and a slight sway breaking the symmetry of the stance. The goddess's expression radiates an aura of sublime majesty—commanding yet enigmatic.

This sculpture retains much of its original high polish, and the contrasts between smooth, bare skin, the incised compression of flesh beneath the breasts, and the decorative drapery motifs add visual interest to the surface. The modeling is superb, and there is a brilliant balance and harmony of volumes and proportions. Part of the original supporting arch can be seen at the back, at the top of the miter.

ML

Donors of Gifts of Works of Art
or of Funds for Acquisition of Works of Art
July 1, 2000–June 30, 2001

Abraham Foundation
Alexander and Helene Abraham
Mr. and Mrs. Warren J. Adelson
Advance Magazine Publishers Inc.
Liz Alderman and Merry Alderman
Harriett Ames Charitable Trust
Mr. and Mrs. Walter H. Annenberg
Ida Applebroog
The Appleman Foundation, Inc.
Pierre Apraxine
Placido Arango
Bernard and Audrey Aronson
    Charitable Trust
E. Nelson Asiel
Ronald R. Atkins
Richard Avedon
Jill Baker
Walter Bareiss
Saretta Barnet
Sylvan Barnet and Will Burto
Will and Elena Barnet
Neal Barr
Bill Barrette and Christine Lilyquist
The Barrington Foundation, Inc.
Sandra Buhai Barz
Mr. and Mrs. Sid R. Bass
Bea and Mitchell Bayer
Ms. Terry Beck
Deborah S. Becker
Renée and Robert Belfer
Jeffrey Bergen
Carmel Berkson
Martha and Robert Bernstein
Robert Gifford Berry and
    Christiane Laus Berry
Beta Research Corporation
Sasha Bezzubov
Patti Cadby Birch
Dolores Dembus Bittleman
Leon and Debra Black
Nelson Blitz
Bastiaan Blok
Anthony and Lois Blumka
William J. Bolger
Anne and Jean Bonna
Virginia Wagoner Booth
Ward and Lynn Botsford
Rose-Helen Breinin and
    Goodwin M. Breinin
Cynthia and Steven Brill
Mr. and Mrs. Kevin R. Brine
Christopher and Barbara Brody Fund
Mr. and Mrs. John S. Brown, Jr.
Mrs. Moreau D. Brown, Jr.
Sally and Thatcher Brown
Mrs. William F. Buckley
Mr. and Mrs. James E. Burke

Mary and Jackson Burke Foundation
Mr. and Mrs. Walter Burke
Lynn H. Butler
Sophie Calle and Olivier
    Renaud-Clement
Douglass Campbell
Mrs. Korda Herskovits Caplan
Cassina USA
Vera Chopak de Champlain
Charina Foundation, Inc.
Judith Childs
Eva and Michael Chow
Jane and Mark Ciabattari
Louis & Virginia Clemente
    Foundation, Inc.
Mrs. Merritt A. Cleveland
Joseph and Barbara Cohen
Karen B. Cohen
Marian and James H. Cohen
The Concordia Foundation
Conner Rosenkranz LLC
Virginia E. Consiglio
William J. Conte
Joyce and Jay Cooper
The Cowles Charitable Trust
Cranshaw Corporation
Mrs. Gisèle Croes
Wendy Cromwell
Thomas F. and Shelia P. Cummings
Paul and Paulette Cushman
Paula Cussi
Courtney C. Dallaire
Frank D'Amore
Natalie T. Darcy
Mavis H. and Philip J. C. Dark
Martin J. Davidson
Mr. and Mrs. Michel David-Weill
Tammis Day
Ruth J. Dean
Ann Demeulemeester
Paul and Gregory Demirjian
Dickinson Roundell, Inc.
Charles and Valerie Diker
The Dillon Fund
The Dobson Foundation Inc.
Doing Art Together, Inc.
Douglas Elliman-Gibbons & Ives
Douglass Foundation
James David Draper
Norman Dubrow
Jennifer and Joseph Duke
Elizabeth F. Eck
Eric Efstathiou
Bequest of Samuel Eilenberg
John B. Elliott through the Mercer Trust
The Charles Engelhard Foundation
Mrs. Richard Ettinghausen

Richard & Rebecca Evans Foundation
Dr. and Mrs. Burton P. Fabricand
Bequest of Mr. and Mrs. Myron S. Falk
Lola Faturoti
Wysse Feininger
Martha Feltenstein
Peter R. Feuchtwanger
Lawrence M. Fields
Mrs. Lawrence A. Fleischman
Martha J. Fleischman
Ernest L. Folk
Nancy Ford
Barbara M. Foster
Mr. and Mrs. John H. Foster
Howard A. and Barbara E. Fox
Gray Foy
Mrs. Daniel Fraad
Franklin Industries, Inc.
Deborah W. Frazer
Evan W. Frazer Jr.
John A. Frazer
David W. and Magda Fried
The Fried Foundation
Adam Fuss
Edward J. Gallagher Jr. Foundation, Inc.
Giuseppe Gazzoni-Frascara
Stephen A. Geiger
The Honorable Sir David and
    Lady Gibbons
Georgina Claudet Gilchrist
Cora Ginsburg
Diana and Carl Giuseppone
Dee Dee and Herbert Glimcher
George J. Gockel
Carol and Arthur Goldberg
Horace W. Goldsmith Foundation
William B. Goldstein M.D.
Mr. and Mrs. Yves Gonnet
Toni K. Goodale
Ms. Elizabeth Marsteller Gordon
John Stuart Gordon
Peter Gottesman
Dan Graham
James L. Greenfield
Mrs. Priscilla Grigas
Christopher C. Grisanti and
    Suzanne P. Fawbush
Steven and Phyllis Gross
Mr. and Mrs. Martin D. Gruss
Gucci
Jeff Guerrier
Gulton Foundation, Inc.
John Gutmann
Alvin D. Hall
Michael E. Hall, Jr.
John V. Hansen
Suzanne and Norman Hascoe

J. William Heath, Jr., and
    Richard A. Heath
Bernhard Heitmann
Heller Incorporated
Frank D. Henderson
The Henfield Foundation
Katrin Henkel
Ms. Judith Hernstadt
Mr. and Mrs. Raymond Herrmann
Neil C. S. Hirsch
Maurine Holbert Hogaboom
Thomas S. C. Holberton Jr.
Mary Tavener Holmes
Roger Holt, M.D.
George L. and Elizabeth U. Hoobler
Mr. and Mrs. Joseph C. Hoopes Jr.
Raymond J. Horowitz
Sir Joseph Hotung
John K. Howat
The Isaacson-Draper Foundation
Mary and Michael Jaharis
Thomas Jayne Studio, Inc.
Lisa Papamarkou Jewell
Alexander B. V. Johnson and
    Roberta J. M. Olson
Frances Claudet Johnson
Anne K. Jones
Lucille and Martin E. Kantor
Bequest of Hertha Katz
Muriel McBrien Kauffman Foundation
Donald Keene
Nanette B. Kelekian
Mr. and Mrs. Stephen M. Kellen
Mr. and Mrs. Robert Keller
Mr. and Mrs. Alvin B. Kernan
Mrs. Joseph H. King
Y. K. Wang King and Kenneth King
Mark E. and Anla Cheng Kingdon
    Foundation
John C. Kirsch
Ruth & Seymour Klein Foundation Inc.
Virgilia Pancoast Klein and
    Walter C. Klein
The Walter C. Klein Foundation, Inc.
Mr. and Mrs. David H. Koch
Robert Koch
Alan W. Kornberg
George P. Kramer
Milton and Fradie Kramer
Mr. and Mrs. Joseph Krieger
Kurtz Family Foundation, Inc.
Robert and Anita LaGamma
Isaac Lagnado
Kenneth S. Lam
Jon Landau
Leonard A. Lauder
Mrs. Jerome Lauren

STATEMENT OF OWNERSHIP, MANAGEMENT, AND CIRCULATION

Publication title: THE METROPOLITAN MUSEUM OF ART BULLETIN

Publication no.: 885-660

Date of filing: October 1, 2001

Issue frequency: Quarterly

No. of issues published annually: Four

Annual subscription price: $25.00, or free to Museum Members

Complete mailing address of known office of publication: 1000 Fifth Avenue, New York, N.Y. 10028-0198

Complete mailing address of headquarters or general business office of publisher:
1000 Fifth Avenue, New York, N.Y. 10028-0198

Full names and addresses of publisher, editor, and managing editor:

Publisher: The Metropolitan Museum of Art, 1000 Fifth Avenue, New York, N.Y. 10028-0198

Editor: Joan Holt, 1000 Fifth Avenue, New York, N.Y. 10028-0198

Managing Editor: None

Owner: The Metropolitan Museum of Art, 1000 Fifth Avenue, New York, N.Y. 10028-0198

Known bondholders, mortgages, and other security holders owning or holding one percent
or more of the local amount of bonds, mortgages, and other securities: None

Tax status: The purpose, function, and nonprofit status of this organization and the tax-exempt
status for federal income tax purposes have not changed during the preceding 12 months.

		Average number of copies during preceding 12 months (Oct. 00–Sept. 01)	Single issues nearest to filing date (July 01)
A.	Total copies printed (net press run)	122,728	126,930
B.	Paid and/or requested circulation		
	1. Paid and/or requested outside-county mail subscriptions	72,658	73,302
	2. Paid in-county subscriptions	32,485	34,222
	3. Sales through dealers, carriers, street vendors, counter sales, and other non-USPS	None	None
	4. Other classes mailed through USPS	7,794	7,750
C.	Total paid and/or requested circulation	112,937	115,274
D.	Free distribution by mail		
	1. Outside-county	None	None
	2. In-county	None	None
	3. Other classes mailed through USPS	180	195
E.	Free distribution outside the mail	6,486	6,080
F.	Total free distribution (sum of D1, D2, D3, and E)	6,666	6,275
G.	Total distribution (sum of C and F)	119,603	121,549
H.	Copies not distributed	3,125	5,381
I.	Total (sum of G and H)	122,728	126,930
J.	Percentage paid and/or requested circulation	94.43%	94.84%